Broadening Our Focus for Healing and Growth

by Enhancing Consciousness and Spaciousness

Chandana Watagodakumbura

To

my parents,

Uncle Sudu and Aunt Stella,

my wife, Inoka, and our two daughters, Manushika and

Methshika,

many other individuals, groups and communities around

the world:

Thank you for being inspirational

in various ways, directly or indirectly,

at different moments and stages of my life.

Table of Contents

Preface

1. Neural basis of learning from an experiential and learner's/educator's inquiry and exploration point of view

2. Inquiry into consciousness

3. Learning primarily informally and experientially

4. Whole-person development, learning and healing

5. Contemplative practices and pedagogies

6. Relationships

7. Final words

Bibliography and other resource links

Author Bio

About the book

Preface

The intention of writing "Broadening Our Focus for Healing and Growth: By Expanding Consciousness and Spaciousness" is to highlight my personal, directly experienced healing and growth journey, the essence of which might be useful to many others. A healing journey is evolutionary by nature and entails a growth journey. The focus of the process can be on any of the two journeys at any given time, or they can be simultaneous. Adversity in the past can inform our future paths, but it does not have to define them. Many transformative stories we hear speak for this aspect. In this piece of writing, I emphasise the intrinsic value of all of our experiences, including the difficult ones, on our evolutionary journeys.

Where we focus our attention can be broadened from ourselves, our immediate interactions, and broader communities to planetary and cosmic levels. The main thesis of this book is that the wider the focus we can maintain, the more the healing and growth effect we experience. To give another indication, an alternative title considered for the book was "Opening Our Senses for Healing and Growth". The growth component includes meaningful connections to our inner and outer worlds, expanding consciousness and spiritual development. It is equally important for our overall well-being for us to reflectively pay attention to our bodily sensations, planetary and cosmic level interconnections and anything in between.

It has been a long journey of exploration, healing, and growth for me. It began in my late teenage years when I experienced a clear mismatch between the notions of human development and growth and education. Growing up as a young child, I learned they aligned well, but real-life experiences showed me otherwise. This fragmentation kept me inquiring, consciously and unconsciously, seeking remedies or an integrated narrative that yielded wholeness and peace. The path of inquiry was not always smooth, safe and skilful. It consisted of moments of frustration, judgemental thoughts, reactivity, outbursts, isolation and alienation. However, it has convinced me that the paths of human development/growth and education do not always have to run parallel or diverge. They can unite in powerful ways, impacting both inner and outer worlds significantly. It is not purely an issue of the education systems that have been put in place, as I conjectured initially. Education is a single but highly influential system in a world of interconnected systems. The need is for deeper, more attuned engagement with the whole of life and experiences, resulting in thriving, flourishing, fulfilment and well-being of all, the whole of the planet, with a unitive narrative.

In the broad topic of healing and growth, I have included six areas I felt were important at the time of writing. They are the neural or physical basis of learning, healing and growth from an experiential and learner's/educator's point of view, an inquiry into consciousness, learning as a dimension of healing, whole-person development, contemplative practices, and relationships. Much research and content related to human development and growth in these areas are emerging. My aim is to be as concise as possible in presenting my overall thesis, emphasising the main topics without getting lost in detail. I have provided a long bibliography and a list of websites for more details. Most of them I have gone through fully or have seen them referred to in other sources encountered. Moreover, I have often attempted to present my subjective direct experiences and intuitive understanding to uniquely reach out to the audience while providing other consilient evidence, including scientific ones, when available.

Thank you

Chandana Watagodakumbura

June 2024

Melbourne, Australia

1

Neural basis of learning from an experiential and learner's/educator's inquiry and exploration point of view

Seeing the brain essentially as a parallel/holistic/systems processor (as a paradigm shift) as opposed to a linear/sequential machine

The human brain and the neural system form a parallel processor comprised of around 90 billion neurons and trillions of neuronal connections. Neurons are the cells that constitute the brain and neural system, and each neuron connects to thousands of other neurons, forming an extensive networked system. These large numbers of neurons and their connections indicate the neural system's vast information-creation, processing, and storage capacities that can eventuate, especially when the right conditions, such as appropriate mind-training practices, are in place. Neurons are also organised and grouped into functional regions in the brain. The interconnected, networked nature of the brain cells and regions gives rise to the possibility of systemic operations or processing yielding outcomes that align with the saying, "The sum is greater than the parts." In a parallel system, individual regions and parts do not function linearly, one after another, in an unintegrated manner. They simultaneously participate in a true systemic co-creation process in an integrative and coherent way. More recent discoveries of neural systems in the heart and gut reveal more overall functional capacities by creating a distributed parallel processing system. What if our decisions are made more coherently through loving and caring inputs from the heart and intuitive feelings carrying our deepest values from the gut? Though they are usually referred to as soft capacities of little significance, they could contribute powerfully and impactfully towards positive outcomes in a contemporary world of many complex problems with multi-dimensionality. The physical structure of the brain and the neural system underscores its complexity and systemic and parallel nature of operation while providing an indication of its potential for approaching the difficult-to-understand notions of consciousness. The above account is a classical scientific and physicalist explanation of the brain function/consciousness. However, based on recent studies, the discussions on the topics can be extended to other areas, such as micro and quantum-level energy and information flows, the complexities of which we do not delve into now.

So, how do the brain, its regions and functional units, and the whole neural system unite to form a miraculous information and energy processing, storage, and communication unit? How can we harness their potential? What can we do to access this immense capacity within each individual? How does the brain's complex parallel and systemic processing capacity signal the possibility of human creativity and flourishing with infinite possibilities? How will it help us to move from a narrow, extractive, scarcity mindset to a broad, regenerative, abundance mindset?

The brain has specialised and lateralised regions. Specialised areas can be found anywhere in the brain, while the left and right hemispheres are the two lateralised regions. These areas add complementary functionalities that support each other for holistic operation. Theoretically, each neuron can be considered a single processor, and many groups of neurons fire or connect together to generate and communicate information each moment. Consequently, the neural system's biological and physiological structure enables parallel, integrative, holistic and coherent functioning. However, it may not always happen due to dysregulated states we may undergo for various reasons. It has the capacity for integrated holistic/self-regulated operation for synergistic functioning, reinforcing the idea that "the sum is greater than the parts." Integration involves the differentiation and linkage of neural networks spread in different brain regions and functional parts. The terms integration, differentiation and linkage are introduced in many publications by renowned author and psychiatrist Daniel Siegel. The two functions of differentiation and linkage support detailed and holistic (big picture) representations and information processing, respectively. A higher degree of differentiation provides a more detailed view of the underlying information while linking information from different or far away regions enables a big-picture representation. Information meant here may not be spatially far away but do so semantically as found in different domains or fields of knowledge.

Interestingly, one of the most popular contemporary psychotherapeutic frameworks known as Internal Family

Systems (IFS), developed by the renowned family therapist and author Richard Schwartz, highlights the need to establish effective communication (linking) among (differentiated) parts of the neural system. These parts are generally known as exiles, managers, and firefighters, who perform different functions based on the individual's past, momentary, and ongoing psychological needs. Communication (linking) that takes place, as that happens within members of a real family, aims to harmonise the functioning (integration/self-regulation) of the whole family, bringing overall psychological well-being. Over time, the communication and harmonising functions can be handed over to the individual's Self (instead of the therapist), his/her essence or higher consciousness, which demonstrates qualities such as compassion, clarity, connectedness, creativity and calm. To get to this level, the client must first be trained to access his/her Self or the essence, or higher consciousness. One of the key features of the IFS model is its non-pathologizing approach to psychotherapy and, in a way, a form of mind-body integration training.

The IFS mode helps individuals to overcome adverse psychological conditions, including trauma, by unifying fragmented parts to wholeness by accessing their Self or higher consciousness. It guides the users to accept all parts following the premise of "no bad parts", as any part has the capacity to be transformed and integrated into the unified whole with the help of the Self. In this context, with the inherent qualities of acceptance and capacity for transformation, the IFS model may be seen beyond a therapeutic model as a path to spiritual development, depending on the extent of its use. We may also conjecture, following the success of the IFS model, on the outcomes possible if we guide our young learners to access their Self or higher consciousness with the qualities of compassion, creativity, connectedness, calm, clarity, etc., at an appropriate age as part of the mainstream education system. Can we also make them more resilient to the challenges of teenage and adult lives by creating a safety buffer with access to the Self in whatever degree possible?

The self-regulation process is generally discussed as consisting of attention, emotion, and cognitive regulation. Each type of regulation feeds the other two types while reciprocally being fed from them, ideally leading to a point of circular balance resulting from the integration process. For example, the eruption of a profoundly emotional feeling can be identified by paying attention to our bodily signals interoceptively. At the same time, their immediate intensity can be regulated with minimal adverse effects by possible processes of reinterpretation, re-contextualisation and acceptance. Put differently, an example of an integrated, holistic neural operation is using our thoughts (cognitive/mental activity) and deep-seated values from our essence or conscience to manage the intensity or reactivity of an emotion. Our deep-seated values or conscience could be formed by a combination of some of our emotions and cognition/mental activity and can be associated with spiritual underpinning. These self-regulatory skills are key topics discussed in the emotional intelligence and self-awareness literature and practices highlighted in contemplative, mystical and wisdom traditions.

A close embodied experience of attention, emotions and thoughts will reveal that they represent some form of energy and information flow within the neural system and body. Thus, the self-regulation process is an activity of balancing these momentary energy flows optimally within the body.

Interestingly and importantly, it is an activity we can train to engage with voluntary awareness and attention. The starting point of a mind-training activity may follow the notion of "where attention goes, energy flows". In social contexts and encounters, the opportunities for co-regulation with those present are as important as the process of self-regulation in maintaining the integrated, embodied balance. In other words, the capacities of the communicating partners to attune to each other will play a significant role in each other's self-regulation process. Attuning is made possible when communicating parties are able to activate their social engagement systems of the neural system, as presented in psychologist Stephen Porges' polyvagal theory. Social engagement systems are activated when no perceived threats are present in the environment. Threats, if present, are perceived through the nervous system's ongoing automatic risk evaluation process, referred to as neuroception. This signifies our spiritual/relational domain functioning and activation, both inner and outer, for our self-regulation process again.

The goal of the integrated, holistic and coherent operation is to allow the most optimal response demanded by a situation to emerge naturally, even in the most challenging situations. It emphasises big-picture processing and being open to information from many regions by maintaining open/choiceless awareness on the go. We relax the whole body and let information and energy be received from all possible sources. This process can be contrasted with a highly differentiated, narrow focus we may have on a piece of information, thought or situation. How can we engage with each momentary experience with such broad openness and curiosity? Fortunately, the capacity for integrated holistic/self-regulated operation develops with practice, and it is a skill that can be enhanced, as studies in neuroscience on contemplative practices have repeatedly revealed. Within this lies the human potential for healing, learning, creativity, expanding consciousness, and the like. Many traditional contemplative and mystical practices and some science-based tools promote the development of these skills. A recurring theme in contemplative practices is slowing down to see the big picture instead of responding hastily, narrowly, or habitually. What mind-training practices help us introduce a gap between a provocative stimulus and the ensuing reaction so as to produce the most optimal response following a contemplation?

A helpful analogy for the differentiation and linkage of neural networks is a person's knowledge of the road networks in a state, province and country. This knowledge consists of regional road networks within specific local areas and the highways connecting faraway places. How easy is it for a person to travel between two distant regional areas if the regional road networks (differentiation) and the highways (linkage) that connect them are well constructed? We may see the significance of highways, without which regional networks stay isolated, devoid of the capacity for connectivity and integration. Returning to the neural system, what if those highways or backbone networks constitute generic but important connecting characteristics of openness (open minds and hearts) and curiosity that carry evolutionary instincts? Moreover, what if they also include loving kindness, compassion, gratitude and the like as foundational connecting tissues of the differentiated (regional) networks? What if we could instil these foundational highways or backbone networks in a child's development trajectory as early as functionally possible while leaving room for developing any differentiated (regional) networks in future?

What would be the outcome of our brain and neural system's non-integrated/ non-self-regulated functioning? Consequences can be critical in some instances. To clarify further, let us turn to some related common analogies. What would be the outcome if a project's team members operated in a non-coordinated/ non-collaborative and non-adaptive manner? What would be an organisation's operation level if its functional units/departments lack coordination, collaboration, agility and co-creation? What are the energy fields created, and what feelings would they generate?

Suppose each neural region processes information and passes it linearly/sequentially to other regions for further processing. Such an operation is usually called the machine model of operation, which performs routine functions at high speeds. Can we achieve a synergistic or the "sum is greater than the parts" benefit from such an operation? Can we benefit from synergistic operation within a business organisation if each department completes its function in its own way and passes it to the other departments? In other words, can we achieve outcomes of the notions of co-sensing and co-creating without having a process of integration? One notable quality of the integration process is that each functional unit uniquely contributes towards a shared, more enhanced objective. The author and psychiatrist, Daniel Siegel, refers to this process as making a fruit salad where the taste of each piece of fruit is preserved instead of a smoothy.

The brain and the neural system together were primarily used as a sequential machine, similar to a typical computer, in the past. Developing learners with mechanistic, linear thinking skills would have been the need following the Industrial Revolution, where humans played a subordinate role to machines in many instances. Things have changed significantly since then, and knowledge work is more prevalent and valued in the information age. This situation has become even more so with the emergence of artificial intelligence (AI) and generative AI (GAI) technologies, where human creativity and relational and collaborative skills leading to co-creation and innovation are much more appealing amidst the automation of routine work. Moreover, an apparent trend is developing currently, moving us to an age of consciousness that pushes us evolutionarily to a higher operational consciousness and energy flows.

Given the brain and neural system's structure primarily as a parallel/systems/inductive processor, it is more appropriate for us to move away from purely linear/deductive models of learning and information processing to the ones that are also based on open awareness that opens us to multiple ways of sensing and receiving information at the same time. Information sensed from multiple sources, internally as well as externally, can be usefully used for making meaningful connections if sensed during the limited time span of the working memory function, the time and space limited holding place for our mental forms such as thoughts and emotions. With this transition, we move away from seeking a quick, narrowly focused and stopgap result to a broader, more creative, integrated, lasting and optimal one. The phenomenon that gets our attention here is the pause required for open awareness. It could just be a fraction of a second pause that could go a long way in breaking free from habitual, conditioned behaviour. Open awareness allows us to broaden our attention and let more related information reach the working memory, including the internal interoceptive signals and intuitive information from the heart and gut. Studies show that the heart and gut carry their own intelligence that can complement the brain's choice- and decision-making capacity with inputs leading to broadness and sustenance.

Based on some quantum physics studies on the phenomena known as entanglement and non-local consciousness, we may even find it difficult to differentiate whether the information our minds receive is internal or external. These phenomena become significant as they transcend the limits of space and time and cannot be explained by the classical physics view of the maximum energy transfer rate as the speed of light. In essence, they provide some evidence of the interconnected nature of the existence of cosmic beings and particles and energy and information transfer among them. Other related areas of study and application are channelling, mediumship, intentions, near-death experiences (NDE), dreaming, synchronicity, telepathy, precognition, morphic resonance and so on. The Institute of Noetic Sciences (IONS), established by the astronaut Edgar Mitchell, the sixth person to walk on the moon, is pioneering similar studies on scientifically understanding complex phenomena of consciousness. IONS has been conducting this work for nearly fifty years now.

We are producing an embodied, holistic response demanded by the situation by being open in a relaxed, full-body, somatic sense. To support such an embodied, whole-person responses, can we afford to pause intentionally on a regular basis in as many interactions, such as listening, speaking, reading, decision-making, etc., for more optimal solutions ahead of speedier results that mostly turn out to be stopgap, short-term in nature, creating more problems in the longer run? Speeds of the process will increase over time once pausing and contemplation become second nature.

Furthermore, our capacities of embodied whole-person presence will enable us to benefit from the emerging technologies of generative AI (GAI) more while equipping us with the much-needed ethical foundations to use them. When the technology moves from AI to GAI, we must move from part-person to embodied whole-person to benefit entirely from the transition.

In the above context, we may appreciate the need to have an open-hearted presence and maintain gut health (or the microbiome health in the gut) for better holistic or whole-person functioning. Studies show the existence of significant neural connectivity between the heart and the brain, as well as the brain and gut, contributing to our psychological and overall well-being. As an important step, what gets highlighted here is the holistic, systemic approach to managing our health and well-being, which is focused on fields such as integrative, functional, energy medicine, energy psychology and food as medicine movement. Interestingly, just as much as our neural system functions as a parallel, integrative system, as discussed above, our overall health and well-being honour a systems or holistic perspective. We may even generalise that everything exists as a system in an interconnected way. The health of every connected part of a system contributes towards its overall healthy functioning. For better or worse, a slight change in a single part or a small group of parts could contribute to a significant shift in the whole system, similar to the self-organisation nature discussed in complex systems theory. The rapid spread of the COVID-19 virus through social systems is a good recent example. The impact of climate change globally, with rapid and extreme fluctuations in recent years, is another. On a related note, some scholars and philosophers are optimistic about shifting global consciousness to a higher impactful threshold level when a critical mass of 10% is reached. This critical mass can be formed by establishing attuned communication among pockets of communities that share the same vision and are scattered around the globe.

Benefiting from the brain's general processing capabilities

Naturally, we can also describe our brain and the neural system as a general processor that performs many tasks in different functional and domain areas. It can be contrasted with a specialised processor that can perform mostly a specific task. As the multiple intelligence theory describes, functional areas include visual-spatial, logical-analytical, verbal-linguistic, interpersonal, intrapersonal, bodily-kinaesthetic, musical and naturalist. For example, often discussed, important relational qualities such as caring, loving kindness and compassion as part of the heart's intelligence could be essential components of interpersonal and intrapersonal intelligence. The body movement and body-mind integration skills developed in practices such as yoga, tai chi, chi gong, various types of dances and movement routines come under bodily-kinaesthetic intelligence. A close look at the above body movement practices will reveal they require bodily-kinaesthetic intelligence to be integrated with other skills, such as intrapersonal and logical-analytical, to some extent. It suggests that areas of intelligence do not present in isolation or mutually exclusive manner but manifest in combinations of other areas in many cases. Or at least they have the capacity to be integrated. Domain areas mentioned above are identified as physical, emotional, mental/cognitive and relational/spiritual.

Our thesis highlights the significance of integrated operation across different functional and domain areas. Usually, in academic environments, we pay attention to and overemphasise the outcomes of mental/cognitive domain processing and tend to disregard the significant influences on it by the other domain areas of physical, emotional and relational/spiritual. This is especially true for learners with grief, loss and a history of unresolved trauma in the forms of individual, collective and ancestral. Similarly, we tend to pay more attention to logical-mathematical and verbal-linguistic functional areas and less to other areas, such as interpersonal, intrapersonal, visual-spatial, bodily-kinaesthetic, etc. It causes the fragmentation of our psyche and moves us away from achieving wholeness, our higher, authentic form of existence required for thriving and flourishing. This a great cause for concern when we yearn for planetary-level solutions to some of the most challenging problems we face to emerge essentially through our wholeness. Encouragingly, more recently developed notions and practices of social and emotional learning (SEL) signify the functional areas of interpersonal and intrapersonal and the domain areas of emotional and relational.

What outcomes would emerge if we can maintain an awareness of the influences from physical, emotional and relational/spiritual domains on primarily focused mental/cognitive domain processing? For example, when we make decisions with an embodied presence, we can let the information and energy entering our mind from all four domains - physical, emotional, mental/cognitive and relational/spiritual –integrate. We let all our senses open with full body relaxation during decision-making. How do various parts of my body, including the heart and gut, feel?

How do I feel emotionally, down, calm or aroused? Am I engaging in perspective-taking, reinterpreting, recontextualising and acceptance? How do I feel relationally or spiritually, inner and outer? How can I maintain balance or an equanimous state while sensing all these? What domain information and energy flows face some vulnerability and require some form of twisting to return to balance? We are not "doing" or judging anything but staying in open awareness to let information and energy flow freely and fill the jigsaw puzzle, world view or a part thereof we have in mind at the time as appropriate. With such reflections, introspections, and contemplations, we have a chance to expand our spaciousness or window of tolerance over time.

Two common opposing human functional areas are analytical/ deductive/ convergent/ reductionist/ focusing on detail and synthesis/inductive/divergent/holistic. We will likely use focused attention practices in the former and open awareness in the latter. Further, they represent more sequential/linear and parallel/holistic processing capacities. It is understood that our left brain hemisphere is more associated with the former type of processing and the right brain with the latter. More importantly, research reveals that capacities in these functional and domain areas can be developed and enhanced with practice. As a natural generic processor, developing as many capacities as possible to some threshold level will help us maintain a balanced operation with a more optimal level of information and energy processing, leading to better, holistic decision-making. For example, we may ask ourselves why we are naturally given two lateralised (functionally different) brain hemispheres. It is for the purpose of complementing each other's functions through integration for a more synergistic operation. To carry out any action with optimal results, we should ideally have a series of alternating self-regulated moments of focused attention and open awareness. The former accomplishes the task while the latter gathers and feeds the required information for a more creative and adaptive output. We alternate between the certainty of focused attention and uncertainty, awe, wonder and curiosity of open awareness. However, it is not uncommon for many of us to act habitually without being aware of where our attention stays and what type of attention it is, commonly referred to as operating in the doing mode instead of functioning in the being mode with awareness/presence.

What difference could it make to our daily routines if we develop a mind state to naturally alternate between focused attention and open awareness at regular intervals, possibly with relatively smaller timescales? Can we maintain an awareness of such changes in our attention? Developing such a reflective awareness continuously is a main focus of the mind-body integration training practices highlighted in contemplative, wisdom and mystical traditions.

Benefiting from the brain's malleability by feeding positive emotions and experiences

The phenomena known as neuroplasticity, neurogenesis, and epigenetics enable us to become increasingly healed from grief, loss, and trauma, creative, see new perspectives, and continuously enhance our worldviews and accessible consciousness. They are relatively newly discovered neural system phenomena. The notion of neuroplasticity, or more formerly experience-dependent neuroplasticity, tells us that our neural connections are malleable and will be changed based on our experiences. Neurogenesis means that we can have new neurons grow throughout life. Epigenetics suggests that our gene expressions (or suppressions) are controlled beyond our genetics by our life experiences. These phenomena can be contrasted with the traditional view that brain resources and capabilities are mostly fixed at birth or could change only in the first two decades of life. A related concept is the development of a growth mindset, moving away from a fixed mindset. Developing a growth mindset becomes a possibility because of the malleable nature of our brain and neural system. A growth mindset can also be considered a change, evolutionary, or transformative mindset. As highlighted in the notion of a growth mindset, the capacity for learning is not fixed at birth or in the early years, and opening our senses to our experiences with embodied presence helps us to learn throughout life, impacting positive physical changes in neural connectivity in our brains. The more positive experiences we can replicate, the better the positive changes we can have in neural connectivity following the notions of "use it or lose it" or "neurones that fire together, wire together". Research studies show that positive psychology practices such as loving-kindness, compassion, gratitude, generosity, etc., broaden our attention and awareness, leading to better learning, creativity, clarity and healing. It follows the broaden-and-build theory developed by the psychologist Barbara Fredrickson. These positive qualities are also understood to emerge from heart intelligence or heart qualities. What would be the possible outcomes in our well-being and daily operations if we engage in these practices more frequently?

Research done by the HeartMath Institute reveals that when heart and brain coherence is achieved through some mind training practices, it generates a positively impacting electromagnetic field around the person. These fields can extend a few feet from the person and positively affect nearby people. Similarly, the study areas of biofield science and psychoneuroimmunology (PNI) explore the presence and uses of such fields. Other related application areas include "mind over matter", the placebo effect, intention setting and visualisations. The main underlying principle of the applications is that even a thought we bring to mind voluntarily can change our neural connectivity. As the renowned author and psychologist Rick Hanson put it, we can use the mind to change the brain to change the mind in a circular and highly impactful relationship. In the context of our discussion, we can reframe it to use embodied presence to change the neural system to change embodied presence. Results and knowledge emerging from various studies as above and the wisdom and mystical traditions repeatedly show the significance of an embodied awareness/presence or embodied centring on the well-being of the individual practising and the others he/she is associating closely. Differently put, we have the capacity and can develop an intention to present ourselves in a whole-person or full-body sense to emerging moments. The more we can bring and maintain these bodily states to being, irrespective of our external situations, the better our relationship with the inner and outer worlds.

Scientific revelations of neuroplasticity, neurogenesis, and epigenetics leave us with agency towards the liberation of the mind by guiding our personal development. How can we use the evidence from these revelations to create ideal conditions of the physical, emotional and relational/spiritual domains for more optimal cognitive/mental domain functioning? For example, how would a broader loving-kindness/compassionate mindset in the relational/spiritual domain create a better psychological landscape or self-regulation/integration capacity for more optimal mental/cognitive domain processing, leading to the sustenance of our life and collective life on earth? Can we use such a holistic approach to make better, more informed and broader decisions with a long-term focus?

Why does persisting with learning and positive habit formation matter despite its initial difficulties?

2

Inquiry into consciousness

Understanding consciousness with an everyday meaning

At a foundational level, consciousness can be considered a system or field of energy and information flow – a fluid or live energy flow model. Depending on how broad we consider the scope of consciousness, it may appear to be organised primarily at the levels of an individual, a locality, the planet and the universe. Though we may have various group-level energy and information flows more prominent and frequent, at the broadest level, as studies on phenomena such as entanglement and non-local connectivity suggest, consciousness is a timeless and spaceless phenomenon, with all beings and particles in the universe connecting across various times and spaces. As some studies, scholars and philosophers put forth, consciousness is the most foundational element of all existence, beyond materialist views. Even matter is considered a condensed form of energy, as presented in Einstein's equation $E = mc^2$. Other supporting evidence to this premise includes the ability of our intentions to have a physical impact on our neural connections, the placebo effect, where our positive thoughts create a physical healing or immunity effect and the use of the notion "mind over matter" in disciplines of philosophy, spirituality and psychology.

The consciousness we hold at an individual level can be considered a worldview. These worldviews are likely to change constantly based on information generated right here and now or thousands of kilometres afar or thousands of years before. Any blockages to smooth energy flow within our bodies can lead to disturbed learning and development and make us prone to ill-health and disease (as in trauma). Journalling, poetry, and other openly expressive creative art forms such as painting, music, and bodily movements can be examples of activities in which we create conditions of open minds and open hearts for a smooth flow of energy and information towards health and well-being. Within an individual, energy and information flow in physical, emotional, mental/cognitive, and relational/spiritual domains.

In what is commonly referred to as a "flow state", we become engrossed with an activity of appropriate challenge contributing towards a useful outcome without even noticing the time passes by. Going by the formal definition of these states, we are likely to have an optimal energy flow level across mental/cognitive, emotional and physical domains, giving rise to moments of high functioning, leading to aha/awe/joy moments of higher consciousness. Usually, during a "flow state", we stay emotionally and physically stable with an adequate interest/curiosity and challenge received in the mental/cognitive domain to stay continuously focused. To enter into a flow state, we can clearly set our intentions to prepare the above domains of energy flow to be stable. In other words, we are in a highly self-regulated state that comprises the components of attention regulation (AR), emotional regulation (ER) and cognitive regulation (CR). We allow for the natural emergence of the moment of "flow" by providing the right conditions for it. We can see each component of regulation feed into the other two components, allowing us to develop a more balanced, equanimous state of mind for optimal operation.

It is interesting to conjecture the role played by the relational/spiritual domain in a flow state in addition to the three usual domains of mental/cognitive, emotional, and physical. A closer look at our direct experiences will suggest that a highly evolved moment in the relational/spiritual domain would bring an additional layer or dimension of supportive, invigorative, connecting energy and information flows to the other three domains. Differently put, when all four domains are highly integrated and ideally set, the resulting state of embodied presence/awareness will enhance the conditions of the flow state function.

What would be the outcome if we were not emotionally regulated? Recall instances in which we were emotionally upset for some period of time. What would be the outcome if we were not regulated in attention? Recall instances in which we struggled to stay focused, such as when we were in a situation of the monkey mind. What would be the outcome if we were not cognitively regulated? Recall instances in which we were rigid and inflexible with our perspectives and found it challenging to shift. What would be the outcome if we were not spiritually/relationally regulated? Recall instances in which we were overly self-critical or held grandiose or narcissistic thoughts. Can we voluntarily create the conditions for flow states to emerge? What situations make it challenging to do so?

Worldviews as partial representations of universal consciousness

Each of us will have a unique worldview at a certain time in life. They can also be understood as a collection of mindsets such as kind, open, generous, grateful and growth mindsets as per the regular usage of the terms. Worldviews are likely to change over time depending on our openness to the evolving stream of consciousness. For example, we may transition from a fixed mindset to a growth mindset or towards a more compassionate mindset by widening our circle of concern over time. We can also consider the role played by advances in information and communication technologies in the evolution of our worldviews through global connectivity.

Our worldviews may also contain major and minor blind spots we cannot see as individuals. They are referred to as shadows and present in the unconscious, which we are hesitant to bring to our consciousness to deal directly with for various reasons. Personal growth and development programs and reflective and introspective practices help us to identify our blind spots or shadows and take appropriate remedial actions to address them. A related topic is individual trauma, bodily memories or parts from which we attempt to disassociate, making us dysfunctional to some degree. Unlike shadows, trauma, in many cases, is likely to be associated with some significant negative personal or collective events in life or other intergenerational causes. As with shadows, the effects of trauma are remedied by integrating traumatic memories or parts with individual consciousness or worldviews to generate growth-oriented, meaningful narratives, as the ones related to post-traumatic growth (PTG).

A related interesting notion introduced by the renowned psychologist Carl Jung is the collective unconscious, which relates to information patterns we are not aware of generally and collectively as a species (may also be as a specific group) but have the capacity to activate, especially in situations of crisis. These information patterns are generally referred to as universal archetypes – universal to the species - and tend to symbolise, in many cases, positive imagery such as "wise old man", "the Self", "Sage", and the like. Jung's work directs us to ponder the untapped potential we possess as a species and the possibility for us to evolve as whole persons by becoming aware of the unconscious and integrating it with the operational consciousness. Interestingly, we come across similar notions in religious literature, such as "the Buddha nature" and "Christ Consciousness." The popular therapeutic model of Internal Family Systems (IFS) also signifies the need to access "the Self", the essence or higher consciousness comprising qualities such as compassion, creativity, clarity, connectedness and so on, to have an enhanced therapeutic healing and developmental effect. On a related matter, we have the phenomena of collective trauma, memories and parts we attempt to keep away as a group, minimising our chances to function fully as whole persons. Again, the remedies come through the integration process of all parts and domains towards wholeness.

The uniqueness of our worldviews, which are more differentiated, conceptualised or manifested views of broader consciousness, gives us value and strength if presented to the world in meaningful, beneficial and creative ways. These unique and more specialised worldviews, formed mainly by pursued interests and lived experiences, give rise to the positive phenomena known as co-sensing, co-creating, co-regulating and co-evolving, leading to a positive collective contribution to the evolution of consciousness or enhanced understanding of reality as is. The common learning model of "one size fits all" practised in contemporary societies forces us all to learn one thing in a conforming way, following a believed-to-be present objective outer reality. It destroys the possible subjective, unique contributions each individual can make. In such a situation, we also lose the inherent deep meaning embedded in co-sensing, co-creation, co-regulation and co-evolving notions. The evolution of consciousness with positive, sustainable manifestations will be constrained. Further, those moments of unique self-expression allow thriving and flourishing while contributing the best to the outer world.

The popular learning theory of constructivist learning suggests that individual learners make sense and meaning uniquely based on their individual experiences – a positive phenomenon if harnessed well. How can we create the conditions for as many human beings on the planet as possible to thrive and flourish, the pathways to which are usually unique? How can we guide individuals, especially the younger ones, to identify their deepest values, essence, and passions so that they can pursue them? How can we instil courage in them for such explorative pursuits? How would such a world look like? How can educational and work organisations contribute towards it?

Conceptualisations make conditioning and may result in rigidity and highly constrained dualistic or black-and-white views in some instances if we are not open to the impermanent, fluid and changing nature of reality as well as its multidimensionality. We require a minimum level of conceptualisation/specialisation/categorisation to strictly hold onto to help us see reality as it is in more connected and fluid ways. Otherwise, we see fragmented pieces of information with strict boundaries, minimal usability, and capacity for interconnectivity, making our decisions unskilful by limiting our views when it comes to social and environmental sustainability. Strictly holding onto fragmented pieces of information leads to highly divisive and detrimental thoughts and social operations, as we have seen in the contemporary world. As a remedy for these negative social situations, many scholars and spiritual leaders propose promoting thoughts and practices of boundless/unconditional/ nonreferential/universal love and compassion. Another useful notion that recently emerged is compassionate latitude, which refers to living with an understanding that, generally, everyone is doing their best with the tools they have to live happily and contribute to the world positively. Even though the above can be difficult notions to practice in all real-life situations, there are no barriers to them being the broad mindsets in which we function all or most of the time. The first and foremost beneficiaries of holding such mindsets are the practitioners themselves, as the right environment for optimal cognitive/mental processing is established. Research studies show that we can widen our circle of compassion through practice. Can we develop a mindset that yields an embodied joy and healing experience when boundless/unconditional/nonreferential/universal love and compassion are practised? How frequently can we generate these feelings of joy and healing? Don't they empower us and give agency in contributing to the positively evolving consciousness of the highly interconnected planet in which we are an important single node, irrespective of our life circumstances? We get humbled, awed and healed when bringing to mind the vastness of the cosmos and consciousness that have existed for billions of years and will continue to exist for many years to come while feeling joy for doing our part, however small that may be, of contributing to the positive evolution of consciousness. Our daily experiences and their associated multidimensionality are brought about by thousands of events, causes and conditions, some more evident while others much less, of upstream consciousness. Some widely discussed causes in the available research studies include traumatic experiences (individual, ancestral/intergenerational and collective) and attachment issues, as in adverse childhood experiences. The attachment studies highlight the significance of young children having a secure base relationship with their caregivers to avoid negative developmental effects, including long-term ones. These studies illustrate our existence's systemic/wholistic/interdependent/interconnected nature, leading to a complexly changing/self-organising nature of consciousness. Given the complex and systemic nature of our everyday experiences, any foundational responses to them should emerge from a mindset of boundless/unconditional/nonreferential/universal love and compassion. How does such a broad/systemic awareness and understanding bring us a higher degree of acceptance, resilience, contentment and healing?

We should attempt to form our basic skeletons of learning with as much raw/generalised information as possible to stay open to and benefit from many other ongoing perspectives we get exposed to over time. When we over conceptualise/specialise/categorise/simplify/compartmentalise information for the purpose of easier understanding within a relatively limited context, we need to make a mental note of the underlying assumptions. Then, we can still stay open to future exposure to related broader information and the ability to make sense of them in enhanced/extended ways. Suppose we don't hold conceptualisations light enough to accommodate future extensions/enhancements/variations. In that case, we are more likely to get stuck in rigidity and have less capability to adapt to an ever-changing and evolving world of consciousness. Conceptualising/conditioning/categorising will help us make decisions quicker and easier with minimal interrogation within a limited context. However, these decisions may not be optimal for yielding more sustainable outcomes in the long run. Conceptualisations are important in implementing and carrying out essential routines in a business-as-usual world. However, seeing them as an end will prohibit our evolution to a positive and sustainable higher level of consciousness.

Levels of reality and identifying patterns of information and energy flow

Enhancing or evolution of consciousness leads to seeing a higher level of reality, or reality as it is, in more connected ways, following the systems thinking approach. We get to see and understand three levels of reality -macro, micro and quantum levels. The macro level relates to what we can see with the naked eye, such as the speed of a car (as described in classical Newtonian physics), while micro and quantum level realities are not visible with the naked eye. Micro levels represent some physical reality, such as microorganisms in the form of bacteria and viruses-related diseases we encounter, the microbiome found in our gut containing trillions of bacteria, etc. In contrast, the quantum level represents the flow of subtle forms of energy and information among cosmic particles (as described in quantum physics). The interconnected or interdependent nature of all life forms and instances on earth is becoming a widely discussed and increasingly accepted notion. These interconnections can be at any of the three levels discussed above. Globalisation/ globalised trade can be an example of macro-level connectivity. The COVID-19 pandemic we recently encountered was an example of micro-level connectivity. Examples of quantum-level connectivity are emerging from various research studies, including the ones in quantum physics, such as entanglement and non-local consciousness.

Identifying patterns of information/knowledge/energy individually and collectively helps us let consciousness evolve and manifest – we also become more creative as we access and directly experience more neural connections and energy flows. Energy flows within our bodies to the places we pay attention to. Attention can have different levels of subtlety. The quieter we become (a higher level of stillness), the subtler and more granular our attention and the access to the forms of energy and information flow. Scientists use the term attentional blink to measure the granularity of our attention. It represents the minimum time required to identify any difference between two successive data items in a series of items presented. Researchers initially thought that attentional blink is a brain's hardwired quality but found that meditation practitioners could lower its value to a significant level following a sustained period of practice.

We can let our external and internal senses receive energy and information by being open – with open minds and hearts (or in a full body sense) – to form lasting embodied memories. To let our hearts and minds open to all our experiences and associated information and energy flows, we need to be curious, courageous and willing to be vulnerable. Some energy and information flows may generate negative emotions and feelings. A general kind/caring, accepting, broader and spiritual mindset will help us to handle this vulnerability. Just as much as we have seen the stillness practices, along with associated calmness and tranquillity, help us retain and store memories, they also help us retrieve the internally modified and stored memories, including the subtleties and nuances sensed. In the presence of phenomena such as entanglement and non-local consciousness, with subtle receptivity, we may be open to other sources of information and energy besides the ones from the five senses and interoception. Future studies on consciousness will give us more clarity.

Retaining information with more connectivity for easier retrieval with enhanced consciousness

Energy flows through our neural system as electrochemical energy, and memories/information are stored as neuronal networks that fire or instantaneously connect together. The more we relate our memories/ neural connections to other existing memories/neural connections when storing, the higher the chances of retrieving with a higher number of related priming or cueing functions (because there will be more priming functions or cues available per memory/neural connection). A pause with an open awareness when taking new information in will help us associate them with more pieces of stored memories after identifying their relatedness. Sometimes, the associations might be weak and need further clarification to strengthen them. Anyhow, establishing a high degree of connectivity among pieces of retained memories helps us to operate at a higher or more fluid level of consciousness. By doing this, we get the opportunity to move away from maintaining rigid boundaries and linear sequencing of the information taken in. Such rigid boundaries and linear sequencing will make the information retained less useful and contribute minimally to enhancing consciousness. Said differently, each new piece of information taken in should be understood first for its own sake as a standalone piece while keeping away from linking to sequential and strictly bounded representations as much as possible. Analogously, each piece of information taken in each mindful moment should be observed for its own sake with minimal judgemental associations with the past and future. This enables us to see the information piece's inherent features in its essence with no add-ons or projections. Pieces of information in their most generic forms will have the highest chance of connecting to other similar pieces of information. In a related matter, researchers have found that a highly connected connectome, a map representing all neural connections in the brain, indicates one's overall well-being.

What differences can we feel if any new information reaching us is held in full-body-relaxed receptivity of open awareness? What connections can this information make with our existing memories?

When we recognise new connections among pieces of information reaching us or held in our memories, they become aha/awe/joy/healing moments as the human neural system has a natural tendency for the characteristic of novelty-seeking. A mindset of openness/ not-knowing/childlike/beginner's mind/curiosity/inclusivity helps create more of these moments of learning and healing in a pervasive manner. With a mindset of openness —open minds and open hearts- we keep away from narrow, judgemental/conditioned reactivity and higher stress and anxiety levels usually associated with the notion of a separate self that diminishes our chances of seeing reality as is, in more connected ways. With practice, an open/not-knowing/child-like mindset trains us to be more comfortable with uncertainty and the associated complexity while guiding us to respond with the highest degree of possibility, minimising premeditated, sub-optimal responses. In spirituality literature, the emergence of such a possibility is highlighted when unconditional/unbounded/nonreferential/universal love and compassion are present. What would be the outcome if as many of us as possible, if not all, pursue this path of openness/curiosity to awe, joy and healing that enables us to contribute to the positively evolving and manifesting consciousness of our universe? After all, we all yearn for happiness and joy in life, and the above is one sustainable, commonly shared path to achieving it. When our basic needs, such as food, shelter, safety connection, etc., are satisfied, we can pursue the path to sustainable awe, joy and healing more purposefully. Put differently, when the conditions are set right, we naturally open our hearts, minds and hands, leading to exploration, connection, compassion and the like. How can we ensure that as many as possible, if not all, receive such conducive environments for thriving and flourishing? How can we extend these conditions of thriving and flourishing beyond individuals to organisations, societies and the planet?

When we are genuinely open to new experiences or even the old ones with new vantage points, life becomes a collection of aha/awe/joy/healing moments, despite some unavoidable difficult-emotion-generating experiences at times. Every moment gives rise to a generative one with an effect of healing that renews our perceptions of reality. To benefit in this way, we can identify a more profound purpose of contributing to positively evolving consciousness by being fully open to the whole spectrum of life experiences. In a way, we develop broader mindsets of acceptance, surrendering, caring, and spirituality while taking action within our circle of influence to address any negative outcomes. The acceptance phenomenon is well supported by scientific studies related to Acceptance and Commitment Therapy (ACT), developed by the renowned psychologist and author Steven Hayes. We tend to abide by the famous serenity prayer: "God, grant me the serenity to accept the things I cannot change, courage to change the things I can, and wisdom to know the difference." This line of thought brings us to the understanding that every experience carries immense potential for learning and development when responded appropriately and purposefully.

How can we use our new experiences in an ongoing manner to refine the narratives we hold? How will this process help us to enhance our spaciousness/window of tolerance?

Hidden patterns of information and energy flow

Renowned quantum physicist David Bohm's "implicate order" suggests hidden patterns of information and energy flow within the broader phenomenon of consciousness. It is possible that an infinite number of such patterns exist, some of which are revealed to us in an ongoing manner through direct subjective experiences as well as scientific discoveries. Interestingly, scientists are showing increasing interest in some historical patterns related to the nature of reality our ancestors experienced directly and understood. Such consilience will help us jump forward in our pursuit of positively enhancing planetary consciousness.

One popular pattern understood and presented in history is Charles Darwin's survival of the fittest theory. He highlighted that the fittest species survive when competing for the essentials. The basis of this theory is the survival of a single species based on their suitability to the environment. This notion may even be applicable to a group of living beings instead of a whole species. At the same time, Darwin has also identified in his work that the most empathic species/groups survive as they give the necessary care for their immature offspring. Based on previous discussions, the latter form is a higher operational consciousness level of cooperation beyond survival needs. In a highly interconnected cosmos, as suggested in the studies of entanglement and non-local connectivity, can there be unseen and non-experienced cosmic or universal patterns that endeavour to sustain the whole cosmos as a single system that includes all its parts or nodes? Do these patterns of consciousness present more strongly beyond individual species or part's survival patterns? Does Bohm's "implicate order" relate to similar symbiotic connectivity among cosmic beings and particles operating at a higher consciousness or subtle, quantum energy level? What was the epiphany of "interconnectedness" and "oneness" that astronaut Edgar Mitchell directly experienced viscerally when returning back to Earth from the moon? What does Greek mythology on GAIA, the personification of Earth as the mother of all life caring for all its children, lead us to conjecture? It is understood that similar notions of our broader interconnected existence at planetary or cosmic levels are also found in several other traditions. The above suggests consciousness as the life force of our existence operating at broader planetary and cosmic levels. In spirituality-related literature, this interconnected nature is commonly referred to as oneness. Do the current extreme climate conditions and outcomes of extreme divisiveness and polarities among groups symbolise warning signals of violating those implicit life-sustaining cosmic or universal patterns of consciousness?

The fact that hidden patterns are waiting for discovery is not surprising when we consider, as an example, the existence of trillions of microorganisms living in our gut and the balance of their spread contributing to our health in subtle ways, including developing our immunity system and contributing to mental well-being – cannot see but can physically experience the changes. It is intriguing and humbling to understand how subtly, and in a significant way, interdependent our health and well-being are with other life forms, including those microorganisms we cannot see with our naked eyes.

How does it feel in the body when we realise that there are infinite patterns of consciousness waiting to be discovered – the humbling vastness and infinite nature of our existence? Who would have imagined the widespread use of mobile phones or mindfulness/awareness/presence practices 50 years ago? How do such broad perspectives and awareness contribute to our contentment, healing and resilience? Once the above patterns are identified, either by direct experience, scientific studies or conciliatory combinations, how can we make good use of them so that the masses benefit relatively quickly? Scholars show great concern for the unfortunate delayed positive impact due to the gap between knowledge and action.

3

Learning primarily informally and experientially

Learning as a dimension of healing by expanding worldviews or consciousness

We can see learning as awe, joy, and healing, generating pervasive processes, and we can apply the concept of life cycle analysis (LCA) to it. To do that, we can encourage young children to identify a broader higher purpose as early as practically feasible. Ideally, it should be broader than associating oneself with a specific career path, which may be too early to predict in a realistic way. We can also highlight and instil in them that learning is pervasive and doesn't have to be restricted to classrooms. With awareness, our lives become the laboratory of learning, with us becoming both test pieces and experimenters/researchers. We can positively expand our worldviews or consciousness with every experience when we learn to respond to them purposefully. The interpersonal and intrapersonal intelligence presented in the theory of multiple intelligence are two key areas we can become aware of in our daily activities while enhancing them throughout life. By doing that, we can endeavour to become our best selves over time and bring our most loving and compassionate selves to the outer world.

We may also be able to overcome some of the aging-related negative beliefs we held for decades, if not for centuries. Suppose we prioritise our individual and collective health and well-being throughout our lives, along with lifelong learning activities in the laboratories of life. Then, can we reverse some of the main issues faced by contemporary resource-intensive healthcare systems? Can we shift the paradigm from long-life to long-health living or enhance our health-span? With age, we have the opportunity to develop broader wisdom and grow to higher levels of consciousness if all our lived experiences are taken as opportunities and responded to appropriately. Interestingly, this notion is the main theme of the recent popular documentary "The Wisdom of Trauma", featuring the renowned physician, author and trauma and addiction specialist Gabor Maté. This vital wisdom and know-how from our age and lived experience can then be passed on to younger generations.

An important question we may ask ourselves is, "What is the essence of learning?". The deceptively simple act of paying attention or persisting/pausing with attention is the key to any learning process. When we engage with the proper leading practices, such as the sustenance of attention and pausing, we let the mind do the magical act of learning. Sometimes, they may create implicit memories (in addition to the explicit ones), and we may not immediately be conscious that learning has occurred. However, these implicit memories will come to conscious awareness with the right cues or priming. The object of attention can be a thought, intention, emotion or an external or internal bodily sensation. Where attention goes, energy flows and neural connections are made. Sustained attention improves clarity using the elongated time of introspection/reflection/rehearsal/contemplation/open awareness. Interestingly, William James, the father of modern psychology, expressed the significance of attention more than a hundred years ago, relating it to "the education par excellence". Knowing its importance, we can also relate to why contemplative, wisdom and mystical traditions emphasise attention-training practices such as focused attention for human and spiritual development.

One of the barriers we may have to overcome is the anxiety and fear generated about what is revealed with a pause. We will have to hold our attention in kind awareness for learning to unravel naturally in any form, sometimes generating difficult emotions of lack of clarity, confusion or uncertainty in the interim. However, in the long run, with practice, clarity will be improved with more connections among the pieces of information and memories revealed. When we continue sustaining attention despite the initial discomfort, over time, we will come to a stage of appreciating the resulting open, not-knowing or beginner's mind with every experience with awe, joy and wonder.

The goal of learning is to become whole or engage in whole-person development. Through whole-person development processes, we actualise as many useful neural system capacities/functionalities as possible, making them efficient and activation-ready for momentarily right cues. Traditionally, learning environments focused primarily on cognitive/mental domain development that concentrates mainly on the multiple intelligence model's logical/analytical and verbal/linguistic intelligence, constricting our capacities for thriving, flourishing and contributing meaningfully to the world. The more whole we become, the higher the level of consciousness we develop and operate, or we become simply more informed, balanced, attuned and responsive in our thoughts, emotions, intentions, actions and synergistic/wholistic operations by bringing our whole complex multidimensional selves to the needs of the momentary situations. When we collectively target and support each other in whole-person-development processes, we begin to function at a higher level of consciousness, individually and collectively, giving us the opportunities to find balanced and sustainable solutions to some of our most complex problems – the so-called wicked problems. The process of whole-person development starts by identifying and putting up its skeleton, which includes the domains of physical, emotional, mental/cognitive, and relational/spiritual. Once the skeleton of the whole-person development process is set up and embodied, individual details of information and energy flow related to each domain found in each experience can be used consciously to meet the demands of every moment. We avoid focusing only on one domain, such as the mental/cognitive domain, without building or being aware of the complete skeleton needed for more inclusive and sustainable solutions.

What would be the outcome if we neglect the physical domain of whole-person development? What would be the outcome if we neglect the emotional domain of whole-person development? What would be the outcome if we neglect the mental/cognitive domain of whole-person development? What would be the outcome if we neglect the relational/spiritual domain of whole-person development? How much does the development in each domain contribute to the developments in other domains? How interdependent are these domains? What would be the benefits of incorporating all four domains of development into a unified whole-person development process?

The physical domain of learning

The physical domain activities that support the notion of whole-person development include having adequate sleep, committing to a healthy diet and exercise and movement practices, maintaining gut health and attuning to our bodily sensations (interoception) on a regular basis. Additionally, they include engaging in embodied learning that forms lasting memories and clarifies our values and purpose. When new contents are introduced for learning, they can be evaluated against the feelings generated in the body at the time for a more embodied learning outcome. Embodied learning that carries pleasant memories such as aha, joyful, awe, and healing moments can be seen as performing the reverse function of storing negative traumatic experiences in our bodies. Trauma, in its various forms, such as individual, ancestral/intergenerational, and collective, is shown to be present in an embodied form as suggested by the renowned psychiatrist, author and trauma specialist Bessel van der Kolk with the term "The body keeps the score", along with a book with the same title. The reverse function may be in the form of "the body keeps the positive score" towards integration and well-being. These positive embodied memories of learning may become an antidote that heals negative traumatic memories gradually, even with small steps.

Adequate sleep, a healthy diet, physical exercise and movement practices, and maintaining gut health improve our health and well-being, enhancing our learning and healing or the whole-person development process. Two important functions of sleep are cleaning up waste in the brain after a full day's activity, thus reinvigorating it for another day's operation and consolidating our memories initiated during the day, an essential learning function. A healthy diet will contribute to a healthy weight and gut with a healthy microbiome, which is vital to overall well-being. Physical exercise and movement routines not only help maintain a healthy weight but also improve emotional and mental/cognitive health. Meeting the needs of sleep, diet, and physical exercise comes under an integrative, holistic, or systems approach to managing health, which, in turn, supports learning and healing, multiplying positive effects on overall well-being.

The emotional domain of learning

The benefits of emotional domain development of the whole-person development process include enhancing spaciousness or windows of tolerance to hold most, if not all, emotions and experiences in gentle awareness, including the difficult ones. This important domain influences or sets the environment for the other domains, including the much-emphasised mental/cognitive domain of learning. It is widely experienced and understood that emotions drive our actions and behaviour. For example, our deep-seated values, essence, and conscience, which we bind to emotionally, work positively for us in this regard. Many related discussions of the emotional domain are done in the areas popularly referred to as emotional intelligence and social and emotional learning. An essential function of this domain is to establish a healthy time gap between emotional stimulus and response that minimises our reactivity while increasing response flexibility or choice.

The mental/cognitive domain of learning

The broad mental/cognitive domain development of the whole-person development process includes becoming open to more perspectives and multidimensionality of the possible solutions, including the ones we consider coming from our opponents or whom we see and consider different to us despite many possible similarities such as common humanity, feelings, suffering, experiences we share. We all operate within practices and systems that have been used for a long time, and we need to collectively sense or co-sense the systems we operate in and become aware of the areas that don't serve us well anymore and produce results no stakeholder wants. For positive change to occur, we need to embark with an understanding of "we are in this together", and we are on a path of positively evolving consciousness of planetary, if not cosmic, scale. When we co-sense the systems we are in, we do so with open hearts and open minds and let ideas and information emerge naturally through free energy flowing through our bodies, with minimal conditioning/compartmentalising. This is more of an inductive process rather than a specific goal-oriented deductive/analytical one, which was the focus of the mental/cognitive domain operations traditionally. Typically, in a deductive process, we make use of the existing information and knowledge to derive a solution within a limited context of already available information. In the inductive approach, we let new, creative solutions emerge from the deepest source/essence by staying calm in open awareness and seeing whether the right jigsaw piece appears to match the puzzle at hand. We may even realise that the definition of the problem may need to change. From another perspective, we let the best solutions emerge in the being mode rather than following through a set of actions in the doing mode towards a more specific solution. Can we have better, more holistic solutions to our problems by staying in stillness with open awareness, allowing solutions to naturally emerge wholly or partially instead of forcefully taking one direction or another, sometimes impulsively?

The spiritual domain of learning

The spiritual domain development of the whole-person development process includes meaningfully and lovingly connecting to our inner selves and others by widening circles to include the whole universe in kind awareness, resembling a higher/divine/cosmic connection to everything. This is a domain that is not historically believed to be associated with learning, but it has been getting some increased attention in the recent past. A deeper engagement in the spiritual domain of learning will help enhance learning in other domains. Additionally, it sets up the ideal background towards a higher future self and away from the perspectives and attention-narrowing notions of separate, solo self, self-criticism, anxiety, narcissism, grandiosity and the like. Spiritual domain development can become the integrating fabric within which the threads of other domain developments can take place ideally and optimally. It is likely to yield more unbiased, clear, less conditioned information that represents reality more closely while more intrinsically motivating the individual to engage with learning deeply. Further, it lays the platform for learners to thrive and heal in the face of adversity, which can be present at any stage of an individual's life. How would broadening perspectives and awareness of the spiritual domain contribute to cognitive/mental domain development, the primary focus area in conventional learning environments?

The spiritual domain learning can include the relational perspectives and feelings of loving-kindness, self-compassion, compassion, gratitude, generosity, appreciative joy, common humanity, forgiveness, higher purpose, etc. It will enhance our spaciousness, healing capacity, resilience and well-being, broaden perspectives and generate hope. Research reveals that the positive psychological characteristics mentioned above can be developed with practice. If we attune to them well and develop appropriate mindsets over time, they give rise to embodied positive learning experiences similar to the experiences of aha/awe/joy. In fact, several resources and research studies are available to confirm the basic innate goodness attributed to human nature. Tara Brach, the renowned meditation teacher and psychologist, even refers to the quality as gold found within, covered by some ordinary clay formed due to individual and collective conditioning. In other words, we can say that the quality of spirituality is embedded deep within us. Our challenge is to let everyone realise and access this great resource amidst various environmental conditioning present to suppress it. Further, embracing the nature of reality or the laws of the nature of reality, such as impermanence, death, becoming ill, and decay, will give moments of contentment, acceptance and surrendering within a caring mindset. The spiritual domain learning can take place in parallel with trauma treatment, if applicable, for enhanced healing effects. As research studies reveal, the trauma of various forms, such as ancestral/intergenerational, individual and collective, are more common in our societies than we would expect. Irrespective of whether one undergoes formal trauma therapy, many will benefit from broadening the perspectives of the spiritual domain learning at various stages of their lives.

When spirituality is understood as making meaningful and loving connections, spiritual and emotional learning domains are addressed in what is commonly referred to as social and emotional learning (SEL), at least to some extent. Spiritual transcendence may have different degrees, and SEL can be a good general starting point at a young age. Those interested in the phenomenon of self-transcendence can pursue the path further as they engage with various life experiences. In general, learning in the emotional and spiritual domains is referred to as developing soft skills, while cognitive domain learning as hard skills. The reasons for the use of the terms soft skills and hard skills may be due to the fluid or imprecise nature of the former and the more rigid, precise, analytical, yes/no type of dualistic nature of the latter. Further, the caring nature of soft skills is usually associated with femininity, while hard skills are with masculinity. Interestingly, the former relates more to holistic processing, while the latter to linear processing. Even though hard skills are traditionally valued more academically and in organisations, there has been increasing emphasis on soft skills in the recent past in all societal environments. Most real-life problems we are trying to solve are much more complex than the ones requiring dualistic right/wrong type solutions. We need the skills and caring mindsets to tolerate uncertainty and complexity for long periods. Our discussions here also reveal how significant both types of skills are in whole-person development, which leads to human thriving and flourishing.

4

Whole-person development, learning and healing

What is the whole-person development process, in essence?

The whole-person development process has the intrinsic nature and practices of inquiring into inner life following the integration of four domain areas – physical, emotional, mental/cognitive and relational/spiritual - leading to identifying our unique ways of being. To better understand this, we contrast it with the traditional learning model, which focuses mainly on the mental/cognitive domain, if not entirely. The whole-person development process also leads to humans thriving and flourishing, with lives expressing themselves more fully in unique, creative, and authentic ways in service to the broader world. It enables all engines of human life to fire in unison or concert. We develop a sense of broad connectedness to planetary and cosmic level existence. Unlike the traditional model, the whole-person development process intrinsically encompasses integrative and healing functions.

Another learning perspective directed towards whole-person development and healing is the integration of unconscious and semi-conscious memories with conscious memories to form more useable, connected/integrated/coherent/holistic memories or narratives that serve our current and future purposes. Conscious memories are more likely to present as integrated than fragmented and narrow ones. A common application of this process of integration is for managing emotionally disturbing memories, such as residues of trauma. Additional mental/cognitive, physical and spiritual domain perspectives or integrated conscious memories may help us to find more balance in the emotional domain as we get exposed to more perspectives of the emotion-generating matters and nature of reality. Unconscious and semi-conscious memories can be accessed by priming or through cues, meditation/mind-training practices of stillness and visualisations.

The whole-person development process as a means of healing from adversity

The whole-person development process intrinsically carries healing from adversity – it may even initiate post-traumatic growth (PTG). It can also be seen as body-mind integration or body-mind-spirit integration, as more specifically referred to in some texts. Trauma and stressful experiences tend to persist more when we disengage the mind from the body (or mind from body and spirit), thus disallowing smooth energy and information flow throughout the body. When our posture supports free flow, such as one that is upright, dignified and alert, the vibratory energy can even be transferred to the earth on which we are standing or sitting uninterruptedly. The spirit or spirituality component mentioned here is associated with the positive relational aspects of learning and healing towards oneself and others.

Adversities prompt us to explore a deeper meaning of our existence and make us more open, content, grateful and generous. PTG, when accompanied by the spirituality domain, makes us appreciate and engage with the services of the greater good, directly or indirectly, such as the work involving services to various forms of marginalised and vulnerable sectors and places in the fringes of our societies. These services can include helping individuals and groups enhance awareness/presence/mindfulness skills to develop lasting and impactful personal growth, well-being and happiness once the basic needs of safety, shelter, food, clothing and connections are fulfilled. Such services will most impact the planet's social and environmental sustainability by strengthening the weakest links in our social and planetary systems. These weakest links have the potential to disrupt or fail the whole system, at least in an ethical sense, if not tangibly, if not addressed timely. Other similar services that focus on the greater good may include engaging in sacred activism, a term coined by the renowned author and teacher of mystic traditions, and community engagement towards inner and outer sacred healing.

As the renowned author and psychiatrist Daniel Siegel highlights with a deeper sense, we may not even have a duality of inner and inter/outer but have an intraconnection to all the other living beings and systems. The notion of intraconnection suggests that all living beings are parts of one extensive system that connects internally to each other, like various systems within our body that function cooperatively towards our overall health and well-being. By embracing this notion, we broaden our perspectives on identity and belonging to the broadest possible planetary or even cosmic levels. Increasing evidence is emerging to support the notions of interconnectedness (or interbeing or intraconnection) and the contributions of the resulting harmonious mindsets to our individual and collective well-being. Interestingly, our ancestors had known the notion of interconnectedness holistically for thousands of years.

Holistic/systemic learning as an essential part of whole-person development and healing

In essence, the whole-person approach to development, learning, and healing must include holistic, systemic understanding or the ability to see the big picture in addition to details. Ideally, the former should precede the latter so as to make learning purposeful with the answer to the question "Why do we learn, and what is the context and relevance?" or a deeper reason/motivation for learning and development. The holistic views develop the skeleton for the details that may follow over time to be linked and compiled as needed, on demand. Details are more fragmented information with a limited/narrower scope without understanding their connection to the whole. We may use the brain's chunking feature that groups information for easy understanding and manipulation to build the initial holistic skeleton. Suppose we highlight detailed information without introducing the holistic skeleton. In that case, learners will find the memories of information short-lived as they don't have a skeleton or foundation to be held onto or get attached to.

Our ancestors appear to have lived at a time when holistic learning/ high-level pattern recognition was more prominent and valued in the absence of more detail-oriented, reductionist science and technology-related tools, learning and practices that are common today. The development of instruments, such as microscopes, telescopes, and other instruments, has led to the latter type of learning. The emergence of fields such as integrative medicine and energy medicine/psychology indicate the shift in our interest back to holistic approaches, still supported by scientific evidence, research and consilience, to some extent in practice areas typically dominated by reductionist science and technology methodologies.

A higher purpose of learning with a holistic focus is to contribute to the evolution of consciousness that benefits all. Learning for the purpose of enhancing our own and collective consciousness can be a courageous and vulnerable act that can be carried out with the inclination of a spiritual mindset, and the practices of open awareness/presence/mindfulness and direct experiencing help immensely in this regard.

Elaborative and distributive rehearsal under optimal conditions for whole-person development, learning and healing

In education-related literature, the term "rehearsal" describes the activity of bringing and holding content in mindful awareness in the working memory. The working memory plays the role of a time-bound stage, in which different contents are loaded either voluntarily or involuntarily for processing, such as making sense and meaning, finding connections, and enhancing clarity. Initial rehearsal occurs when information enters the working memory for the first time or learning some contents for the first time, and any subsequent retrieval of these memories becomes secondary rehearsal. Elaborative rehearsal occurs when learning contents are held and processed in the working memory for an extended period to gain greater clarity, simplification and consolidation. When information is retrieved to working memory for rehearsal after a reasonable time gap from the initial rehearsal, it is referred to as distributive rehearsal. Research shows that elaborative and distributive rehearsal types significantly impact positive learning outcomes and memory consolidation. The integrated, clarified, and often meaning-simplified memories created in the short-term working memory will have a better chance of being converted into long-term memories. Affirmations, visualisations and intention settings are examples of elaborative rehearsal that occurs outside usual learning environments and contents and is usually found in personal or spiritual development contexts. These practices can also be performed with distributive rehearsal. Further, these types of rehearsal can also take place more specifically in association with the emotional domain in therapeutic healing sessions, in the presence of a therapist in many situations. These instances could relate to healing from trauma, grief or loss.

We can perform elaborative and secondary distributive rehearsal by bringing contents to the working memory to make sense and meaning, contextualising, re-contextualising, improving clarity, and consolidating memory through integrative and pruning or letting go functions. When clarity is improved, unwanted memory traces that do not serve well, make sense and meaning or relate well get pruned. At the same time, some new meaningful connections are identified, thus enhancing the simplicity of what used to be more complex and fragmented pieces of information. An example of improving clarity, simplifying and making sense of past difficult emotions could be, as the saying goes, letting go of the hope for a better past, which is not pragmatic but hopeful of the best possible overall future outcomes of a compassionate nature. Such themes are the primary use in the therapeutic healing approach known as solution-focused therapy and practices of unitive justice.

We can alternate between open awareness and focused attention practices during a rehearsal exercise as needed. An extended period of rehearsing (elaborate rehearsing) or slowing down of the activity (as if we are blessed with an infinite amount of time) can lead to enhanced understanding and clarity with more connectedness among contents, leading to creativity, insights and expanded consciousness. Another way of looking at this slowing-down process that enhances learning and healing is having a pause from an act of hurriedly doing in habitual/automatic ways to engage in an activity of contemplation, as highlighted in ancient wisdom and mystical traditions. This slowing-down, pausing or contemplation process allows us to access information and energy flowing within the whole body at a higher granularity or resolution level, revealing subtle details, including the subconscious and unconscious.

Further, during the rehearsal process, we can experience the feeling or vagal tone – positive or negative - in the body. A new aha/awe moment with a positive tone will give us a more embodied understanding of the contents or situation, along with the positive, stronger neural connections they make. With openness and curiosity, we are likely activating our highly connected salience neural network with these positive encounters, thus creating embodied knowledge. The salience neural network is activated when we identify a piece of information sensed as important. A disproving negative feeling tone may give rise to the tagging of the contents with curiosity/an urge for further clarification. To yield fully embodied understanding and healing involving the whole person, we may let deep stillness integrate the four domains of learning and healing – physical, emotional, mental and relational/spiritual. Such integrated, embodied learning is likely to expand our intuitive repertoire, which will be instinctively called to our working memory in the future when related priming functions take place or appropriate cues appear. It is interesting to verify when integrated, embodied learning and healing occur under optimal and balanced conditions, as above, whether a biofield is created with a full bodily resonance/coherence as referred to in some related literature.

Guarding our natural, intuitive responses to contribute to the greater good and broader social and environmental sustainability

When we allow embodied memories to be formed with information and energy flows that enter via our internal and external senses, these memories could become part of our natural or intuitive responses in future. In this situation, how can we make sure our intuitive responses contribute to the greater good, are broadly acceptable to the planet we live on, and abide by our deepest values perceived in a whole-person sense? In order to achieve this goal, we have to make sure that the information and energy we take in is screened or tagged by our deepest values and other harmony and sustainability-promoting fundamental filters and tags such as the notions of interconnectedness, empathy, compassion, loving-kindness, gratitude, joy, perspective-taking and the like. This filtering process should occur for internal and external sources of information, energy or vibrations. When these filters and tags are well-tuned and put in place to emerge naturally, we can let our intuitive thoughts and ideas emerge freely without any restrictions or blockages, irrespective of the sources of origin, in a highly interconnected universe. In a world of information overload, misinformation and disinformation, we must be diligent in monitoring what information, energy or vibrations we let in, as traces of them will be reflected in our future responses to social situations.

Outcomes of focusing only on the predominant mental/cognitive domain of learning, disregarding whole-person perspectives

What would be the individual and social outcomes if we focused only on the cognitive domain of learning, as has been a long-term practice in the past? Stressful work conditions and home and social environments lead to less-than-ideal intrapersonal and interpersonal relationships and well-being, resulting in grievous and traumatising experiences. We tend to live in our heads, resulting in automatic, habitual functioning instead of full-bodied, whole-person receptivity and holistic, more attuned responding. Further, less human thriving, flourishing and creative outcomes will be present, along with minimal contribution to the positive evolution of consciousness to higher levels. In short, we will be less directed towards social and environmental sustainability. We might progress technologically and scientifically in a narrow, single-dimensional way while living incompatibly in a reality that is essentially complex, systemic and multidimensional. There is little or no holistic understanding and progress with many fragmentations and divisiveness. Is that what we see mainly in the current world that lacks focus on physical/embodied, emotional and relational/spiritual domains of learning and healing? Focusing merely on the cognitive/mental domain of learning will yield rapid one-sided results without a balance, sustainability, broadness, inclusivity, a holistic nature and a strategic vision.

Significance of alternating between focussed attention and open awareness when engaging in real-life encounters as whole persons

Alternating between open awareness and focused attention helps us learn, enhance understanding, accomplish tasks and heal in more ideal, comprehensive and sustainable ways. Open awareness brings us more perspectives on problem-solving and life as a whole, while focused attention guides us to take action in mindful ways by overcoming automatic, habitual functioning. It is a more conscious way of living as many moments of life as possible. Habits, understood to utilise fewer neural resources than learning new tasks, are a helpful way to preserve resources for more ongoing learning. However, we need to make sure we re-evaluate our habits regularly to verify their applicability to the task at hand in the presence of ever-changing landscapes of our lives.

Open awareness needs open-heartedness and open-mindedness, an attitude of not knowing/childlike/beginner's mind and vulnerability. A truly open mind may not be possible without the receptivity of an open heart. In a way, it is an openness in a full-body, whole-person sense. With that comes creative ways of seeing solutions to complex problems with a multidimensional, broader focus via all available information and energy sources. We have neural systems in the heart and gut, not only in the brain, and we can be receptive to energy and information flow from our whole body with the benefit of getting more accurate, interconnected/integrated and coherent/resonant information and energy. The heart and gut can be seen as another embodied layer of the distributed parallel-processing system in addition to the layers formed by billions of neurons in the brain. The distributed parallel-processing system given to us by evolution invites us to more embodied, holistic, and integrative reception and processing of diverse forms of differentiated energy and information that reach us.

Ideally, we should be able to extend our whole-person presence and receptivity to as many social situations as possible. When any significant threat is absent, we can activate our social engagement neural network to attune to others with deeper connectivity, as suggested in the polyvagal psychology theory. It says that our neural system performs an activity known as neuroception – continuously scanning the environment unconsciously to see whether it is safe or threatening. It is interesting to know whether we can use the same scanning capability to be more receptive, in a whole-person sense, to the information and energy flowing around us when any identified threat is absent.

5

Contemplative practices and pedagogies

The essence of contemplative practices and pedagogies as found in wisdom and mystical traditions

The interest in contemplative practices by the general public and media has grown significantly in the last two to three decades due to their favourable practical applicability in many disciplines and fields. As a result, the essence of these practices has crept into the educational arena, too, as contemplative pedagogies. The origins of contemplative practices are found in wisdom and mystical traditions that go back thousands of years. At a fundamental level, contemplative practices promote a pause with introspection or self-reflection when dealing with information or energy flows within and without. Such a deep and elongated engagement with information and energy flows within and without is found to be the starting point for more meaningful, ethical, loving and wise connections to ourselves, those around us, broader communities, the whole of humanity, the living world and nature. According to most wisdom and mystical traditions and some studies projecting them, this outcome appears universal to all human beings and intrinsic to human nature. When we are open to the inquiry of our direct experiences with utmost self-honesty, authenticity and diligence, we realise that we are only a single test piece or node in the universe with millions and millions of similar nodes sharing similar experiences. We embrace our common humanity or a "just like me" attitude along with all the joys and sorrows associated and get inspired to use our agency individually and collectively to whatever degree possible to improve the current state of the human and planetary condition.

When we refer to contemplative practices, meditation is the most commonly used activity with which we are familiar. In meditative practices, we attempt to still and steady our minds and bodies, commonly by holding an object of focus in mind, non-judgementally and voluntarily observing the thoughts and emotions passing by with open awareness, or consciously wishing ourselves and other living beings goodwill. But there are many other more regular activities beyond the meditation cushion that we can use and integrate as contemplative practices. They include listening, reading, journaling, body movement practices, artwork, poetry, creating and listening to music and the like. The difference in the contemplative approaches to these practices is the more conscious, deeper engagement in them with self-reflection without a sense of hurriedness. All these practices can be more readily integrated into an educational setting using appropriate and thoughtful pedagogical practices.

All of the above contemplative practices, and many related others, train us to better self-regulate our minds and bodies, which includes attention, emotion and cognitive regulation. We become skilful in sustaining our attention by overcoming distractions, responding better to diverse emotions by overcoming reactivity and habituation and opening up to diverse (if not all) perspectives by overcoming the discomfort associated. Contemplative practices invite and support us to be present with our whole, embodied selves in every emergent moment. They help us to bring balance to the four domains of physical, mental/cognitive, emotional and relational/spiritual. Over time, we develop an increasing degree of spaciousness or equanimous states of mind, which is fundamental in staying balanced and steady amidst the ups and downs of our lives. Why shouldn't we equip our future generation learners with these vital generic life skills leading to human thriving and flourishing? Why shouldn't the methodologies and techniques to develop them be part of the pedagogies used, irrespective of the field of study?

Contemplative practices and their guide to inner experiences

Contemplative practices make us more appreciative and receptive to our inner, directly experienced worlds. In doing so, they help us to have a more balance between inner and outer information and energy flows. We become more open and receptive with feelings of curiosity and awe to the external information and energy flows while accepting and expressing internal information and energy flows more consciously, steadily and calmly with minimal reactivity and habituation. There will be less blockages to information and energy flows within and at the boundaries of our bodies. Suppose we attempt to force a third-person objective reality into us in a dehumanising manner, disregarding our inner realities of who we are, in essence. In that case, they will have high friction in between and less chance of integration. One possible way to overcome this friction is to map the context or storyline of the outer objective reality to our internal context or storyline. If there is a mismatch between them, we can make a mental note of the difference to revisit and explore it when more information is available while embracing the prevailing uncertainty in between with awe and wonder and without unauthentically hurrying to an agreement to avoid the associated discomfort. Viewing from another angle, contemplative practices help us to express ourselves in a more holistic, fully receptive and embodied (somatic) way as a result of the integration of the outer and inner information and energy flows. We move away from passive consumers of a third-person objective reality to active contributors to universal or cosmic consciousness, however small it may be.

Contemplative practices and their applicability to healing from loss, grief and trauma

Open-hearted and open-minded inquiry, curiosity, awe, wonder, humility, and the result of expanding consciousness deeply associated with contemplative practices lead us to heal from our past wounds and traumatic experiences. With open and deep engagements of new inner and outer information and energy flows, we are taken out of habitual ruminating cycles of the past while opening us to new perspectives and possibilities. By carefully selecting these new information and energy flows, we can let them cast deeper, enriching neural pathways in our neural systems while allowing the non-serving pathways of the past to subside over time. In general, by broadening our focus and opening our senses to universal truths and realities, as that happens in contemplative practices, we give ourselves a better chance for healing. Our personal mishaps may appear more tolerable in the vastness of the energetically interconnected universe and some of the most significant challenges to life in it. Emerging research points us to greater effectiveness of broader spirituality and heart-based information and energy flows when healing from past negative experiences. The more exposure to these new rejuvenating experiences, the better the overall outcomes would be. Contemplative practices in their diverse forms can be an additional toolkit or dimension to support treating various forms of trauma. They have the potential to put those who faced adversity on a path to post-traumatic growth, as revealed in research studies. Ongoing contemplative practices make us more resilient to adversity – the quicker bouncing back quality -and additionally act as a buffer or shock absorber during adversity. It is as if we buy an insurance policy for unavoidable and unexpected challenges of life.

Contemplative practices and their traditional minimal use in STEM fields

Traditionally, contemplative practices and pedagogies were minimally integrated with STEM education disciplines that emphasise distant, dehumanised, dualistic objective third-person knowledge. In them, the main focus is on mental/cognitive domain functioning. In contrast, we appreciate more open, subjective, creative, directly experienced and fluid forms of information and energy processing in contemplative practices and pedagogies. Such subjective but unifying and unique information and energy processing, present through human thriving and flourishing, will lead to co-creations and innovations guiding the evolution of humanity and consciousness. In fact, this could be the only path to the evolution of individuals, societies, systems, disciplines, humanity, planetary conditions and consciousness. Even the hypothesis of an objective or STEM field research work should ideally emerge with meaning and purpose from a subjective, direct experience.

6

Relationships

Why do relationships matter?

Essentially, we have relationships with ourselves, immediate others, the wider/outer world extending to the planetary and cosmic levels and the whole of nature. A closer look will reveal that all our experiences are associated with some form of relationship(s), inner and/or outer. As a result, learning how to self-regulate energy and information flows within our relationships in mutually beneficial ways is of great significance for our individual and collective well-being and happiness. Ideally, we will have to bring conscious/mindful living to every moment of our existence to achieve this goal.

Relationships – how do they contribute to the process of whole-person development?

How do relationships impact our learning and healing towards a whole person? Our relationships begin with the intrapersonal inquiry we have with ourselves. Self-awareness and self-compassion are widely discussed practices that help us to develop healthy intrapersonal skills. With self-awareness, we learn to reflectively notice our bodily sensations, including the ones generated in the body by our emotions when they arise. Other types of notable self-knowledge include our deepest values and purpose, though they may evolve over time. Self-compassion helps us develop a kind and accepting mindset towards ourselves and reflections that include the vital notion of common humanity: we are only a single node in the fabric of humanity facing difficult situations. The third component of self-compassion is mindfulness, besides self-kindness and common humanity. We can develop the courage, the yang part, in addition to the soft yin nature, to face difficult situations by bringing to mind the learning the situation gives and the opportunity present with this learning to be used for the common/greater good sooner or later. Such an approach to adversity gives us a higher purpose beyond ourselves, expanding our consciousness simultaneously. As part of being kind to ourselves, we can engage in activities that rejuvenate us regularly within our daily routines. They could include spending time in stillness, solitude, introspection or reflection to connect with our essence, the inner core.

The outer or interpersonal aspect of the relational/spiritual domain of learning and healing can be broadly described as making meaningful and loving connections with the external world, starting from immediate others and extending to planetary and cosmic levels. The challenge many of us face is not to exclude any extent of ourselves (the intrapersonal aspect), immediate others and broader communities up to planetary and cosmic levels from our kind awareness to facilitate reciprocally well-being-promoting practices of all-inclusive, nonreferential/universal/unconditional loving-kindness and compassion. What we highlight is not an act of balancing different extents but a deep appreciation and experiential feeling of what is real, our intraconnected (or interconnected or interbeing) nature of existence – we are as parts of a whole. Conversely, primarily, both relational/spiritual and emotional domains of learning and healing, the binding and integrating thread of the tapestry of learning and healing, are directly impacted by our interpersonal relationships. Consequently, we can see that our relationships indirectly impact our cognitive (and physical) learning domain. Co-regulating using our social engagement system of the neutral system and body will help us maintain the ideal environments for our learning, healing and development. With the skills of attuning, co-sensing, co-regulating and co-creating, we get the opportunity in every interpersonal interaction to facilitate each other's co-evolving to their unique, best possible selves. Nonviolent communication, intersubjectivity, empathic listening, active and deep listening and mutual awakening are widely discussed practices and topics in this context. It is interesting to note that learning, healing, expansion of consciousness and spaciousness, becoming whole, self-expansion/-transcendence, and awakening are naturally emerging sequences of evolution when engaged appropriately. The learning highlighted here relates primarily to intrapersonal and interpersonal areas. Engagements in meditation, contemplative practices, introspection, reflection, and various therapeutic sessions are used to journey through the path to healing, self-expansion and awakening. The therapeutic sessions can also be in the forms of community, shared holding places and psychedelic-assisted therapy, an area that has gained significant interest in the recent past and many ongoing research studies conducted. The use of psychedelics is shown to expand consciousness or create altered states of consciousness, thus giving the client a glimpse of an unprecedented broadening experience and possibilities even with a single instance of use resulting in a lasting impact.

Co-sensing, co-regulating, co-creating and co-evolving require openness and contribute to the healing of a traumatised world with widespread instances of childhood, ancestral/intergenerational and collective trauma, non-secure attachment issues, loss and grief caused by death and separation of close ones, etc. These activities can also be done more effectively in a supportive community gathering by creating what we refer to as a shared, sacred holding space to handle individual, ancestral/intergenerational and collective trauma and other impacts of loss and grief. Difficulties our ancestors underwent and their deaths may have caused can be brought to our awareness in order to integrate possible unconscious, semi-conscious and fragmented memories into our full consciousness and meaningful narratives. By doing this, we reach a deeper level of acceptance with unified consciousness on matters we may have little control over. We also get to appreciate the timeless and spaceless nature of our living consciousness that will continue to impact our evolution to a higher level of human development, personally as well as collectively.

Interconnected relationships in an ultimate sense

In an ultimate systems concept of connectedness, everything is connected to everything else. Many of these subtle connections are observed and experienced at the quantum or subtle energy field level, as presented in entanglement and non-local consciousness studies and expressed in wisdom and mystical traditions. Wholistic learning and healing covering the four domains mentioned previously – physical, emotional, mental and relational/spiritual - gives us a chance to directly experience the nature of the vast interconnectedness, interdependence or web of life we live in. Such an understanding develops a great appreciation of the positive psychology notions of loving-kindness, compassion, humility, gratitude, generosity, gracefulness, forgiveness and the like in relation to whole life on our planet, promoting appreciative thoughts of diversity and inclusivity and our broader identity and belonging. All life forms contribute varying degrees to the evolving cosmic level consciousness by transmitting energy and information bi-directionally. Even matter is considered a condensed form of energy that contributes to cosmic consciousness in a similar way. Renowned cosmologist and author Jude Currivan even goes on to speculate the occurrence of an orderly Big Breadth instead of the random Big Bang theory of creation to highlight the conscious nature of cosmic events. In a similar vein, the renowned late physicist David Bohm presented the notion of "implicate order" to highlight the somewhat obscure, interconnected (more specifically, the holomovement or undivided wholeness in movement), orderly nature of the existence of universal particles and consciousness. The notion of holomovement is very similar to the ancient Buddhist representation of an Indra's Net, a network of jewels (metaphorically representing living beings) where each jewel reflects the glitters of all other jewels in the whole network.

The above notions suggest the ongoing endeavour of the cosmic consciousness evolution towards sustenance despite the challenges of the era of the Anthropocene. The presence of many groups of people worldwide engaging in preserving planetary-scale, holistic health is a macro-level example of the presence of orderly consciousness, irrespective of the original sources of such initiations and consciousness. We feed into cosmic consciousness and are fed from it, sometimes in difficult-to-see and comprehend subtle ways. This line of thinking and experiencing brings us to the notion that "we are the consciousness" and "we are the oneness of the fluidity or flux of consciousness" that flows in a spaceless and timeless manner. We all are nodes of fish swimming in the flux of consciousness while giving and receiving energy and information to and from it in diverse forms. Every life instance that has lived in the past and will live in the future will contribute to the evolution of consciousness in direct or indirect ways. Developing such a broader understanding and mindset of belonging and attempting to experience it directly whenever possible guides us to transcend the contrived and constricted notion of a separate, solo self. Why would we buy into such a line of thought or mindset if we cannot see it with our eyes? What benefits will it give us? It will relieve us from focusing on narrowing mindsets of the unhealthy spectrum of self-criticism, narcissism, grandiosity and the like that result in prolonged stress and anxiety while at the same time broadening our focus to positive psychological characteristics. It sets up the conditions for us to become better energy and information transmitters, receivers and processors, enhancing clarity and meaning and establishing new connections of memories and information we hold and process.

Positive psychology characteristics that lead to a broader mindset of agency and abundance

Positive psychological characteristics such as loving-kindness, empathy, self-compassion, compassion, appreciative joy, gratitude and generosity, gracefulness, forgiveness, etc., are shown to broaden our attention, leading to our individual resilience, well-being, fulfilment, thriving and flourishing, as well as societal-level collective resilience. The broader the extent of their inclusion up to planetary and cosmic levels, the better the outcomes. They give us a mindset of agency, abundance and contentment to engage with the world positively while keeping us away from a focus-narrowing scarcity/lacking mindset. When our basic needs are satisfied to a comfortable level, we have the agency to engage in inner development processes guiding us towards reciprocal health, well-being and happiness, leading to better outer contributions. As research studies signify, intentional practice can develop these positive psychological characteristics over time.

Developing resilience and well-being can be essential outcomes of our holistic learning and healing or the whole-person development process. We can understand becoming resilient and developing well-being as a function of multidimensionality that includes presence/mindfulness, self-awareness, empathy, compassion, higher purpose, an understanding of common humanity and interconnectedness of life where we become a single node of the cosmic system in which each individual node is striving to survive, thrive and flourish and be of service to the whole. Research studies by the Centre for Healthy Minds, founded and led by renowned neuroscientist Richard Davidson, specifically identify four pillars of awareness, connection, insight and purpose (ACIP) contributing to our well-being. Individually, our subjective embodied direct experiences will guide us in understanding the nature of reality, undergoing inner development and providing a unique outer service. In a mutually beneficial and empowering relationship with others, we can hold each other compassionately accountable for becoming their best possible whole selves. What could be the possible outcome if we appreciate such a notion at the grassroots level, however esoteric it may appear?

7

Final Words

Healing and growth processes can take place simultaneously. Ideally, they should so as to promote and expedite a person's holistic development and well-being. Since loss, grief, and trauma of various forms are not uncommon events in our world, it is imperative we understand the multitude of reliable and proven healing (and growth) activities and processes available to us as parents, caregivers, and even as individuals. Adverse life situations should not define who we are; instead, they can inform our future trajectories.

Even though the physical basis of learning, healing, growth and expanding consciousness was presented by delving into some areas of neuroscience. more recent quantum-level studies point to energetic connections and practices that explain the above phenomena more nuancedly. Interestingly, these energetic practices have been used for millennia in wisdom, contemplative, and mystical traditions to enhance personal and collective social well-being. Currently, available scientific tools and techniques provide some means of verifying some of the timeless wisdom that prevailed. The brain and the neural system are presented as having a holistic, systemic function supported by their structure, moving away from conventionally understood and promoting linear functioning.

An inquiry into consciousness reveals that it is a conscious energy field in which we all swim. It is fundamental to planetary and cosmic existence and appears to consciously work for the sustenance of the universe with some order. Even physical forms are condensed forms of consciousness. The energy flows of consciousness can be judiciously selected and used to self-regulate our inner worlds for equanimous states of mind as well as to establish loving and compassionate relationships with the outer worlds, extending up to the whole cosmos. Expanding our consciousness to hold all our experiences with spaciousness, including the difficult ones, guides us to be resilient and purposeful in life. Every life experience has an inherent potential to direct us to a higher level of consciousness, especially in developing spaciousness and spirituality. We can use these experiences throughout our lives for learning, growth, and even transcendence.

Every emergent moment gives us the opportunity to be present with a whole-person perspective that encompasses physical, emotional, mental, and spiritual domains. If we leave out any of the domains, we may not be fully present and attuned to the moment, resulting in substandard functioning and decision- and choice-making. With practice, over time, we can bring our whole-person, embodied, heart-centred, loving, compassionate and inclusive presence to our every experience, yielding positive inner and outer world energy fields and empowering us and others to be present with our unique, thriving and flourishing selves. It is of great significance that our education systems at all levels focus on all four domains of learning and consciousness to bring forth the whole-person development of learners, better preparing them for complex, ever-changing environments demanding our undivided attention and wholeness.

Contemplative practices, including pedagogical ones, are gaining widespread attention and recognition. In essence, they direct us to be conscious and reflective in all our inner and outer encounters while keeping us away from habitual, conditioned, premeditated behaviours. We are prompted to appreciate stillness and slow down regularly to gain a higher degree of clarity, optimal inner and outer functioning and collective well-being. Contemplative pedagogies can be a starting point to introduce a broader, in-depth, richer, enlivened form of existence for all. With them, we emphasise the processes, contexts, and connections over content, giving rise to the co-creation of knowledge with shared value and unitive narratives.

All our experiences can be seen as a form of relationship, either to ourselves or the outer world extending to the whole cosmos. Relationships are a form of energy field we related in the inquiry on consciousness. Self-awareness, empathy and social awareness are essential ingredients in the field of relationships. At the highest level of consciousness, all particles and beings are connected to all the particles and beings in the universe. Unconditional/nonreferential/universal love, compassion and compassionate latitude are the ultimate threads of sustenance for the fabric of life. The power of the presence of such a life force or heart-centred coherent field cannot be overemphasised. It will yield a rippling effect, guiding us away from the poly-crisis situation that is currently being faced collectively at the planetary level. The absence of the same can be equally destructive, individually and collectively, as shown by some historical events.

Bibliography and Other Resource Links

Almaas, A. H. (2023). *Nondual Love: Awakening to the Loving Nature of Reality*. Colorado, USA: Shambhala.

Analayo. (2024). *Abiding in emptiness: A guide for meditative practice*. Massachusetts, USA: Wisdom Publications.

Anderson, F. G. (2024). *To be loved: A story of truth, trauma, and transformation*. Wisconsin, USA: Bridge City Books.

Andreas, C. (2024). *The Wholeness Work Essential Guide - Level I: Healing & Awakening: 1*. California, USA: Real People Press.

Armstrong, T. (2008). *The human odyssey: Navigating the twelve stages of life*. New York, NY: Sterling Publishing.

Armstrong, T. (2011). *The Power of Neurodiversity: Unleashing the Advantages of Your Differently Wired Brain*. Boston, MA: Da Capo Lifelong Books.

Aron, E. N. (1997). *The Highly Sensitive Person: How to Thrive When the World Overwhelms You*. New York, NY: Broadway Books.

Aron, E. N. (2010). *Psychotherapy and the Highly Sensitive Person.* London, UK: Routledge.

Baars, B. J. and N. M. Gage. (2010) *Cognition, Brain, and Consciousness—Introduction to Cognitive Neuroscience* (2nd ed.). Cambridge, MA: Elsevier.

Barbezat, D. P., and M. Bush. (2014). *Contemplative practice in higher education: Powerful methods to transform teaching and learning.* San Francisco, CA: Jossey-Bass.

Battaglia, M. (2002). *A Hermeneutic Historical Study of Kazimierz Dabrowski and His Theory of Positive Disintegration.* PhD Thesis at Virginia Polytechnic Institute and State University, Blacksburg, VA, USA.

Bauer-Wu, S. (2024). A future we can love: How we can reverse the climate crisis with the power of our hearts and minds. Colorado, USA: SHAMBHALA.

Baxter Magolda, M. B. (2017). *Authoring Your Life: Developing Your INTERNAL VOICE to Navigate Life's Challenges.* Virginia: Stylus Publishing.

Beale, R., and T. Jackson. (1990). *Neural Computing—An Introduction.* Bristol, UK: Institute of Physics Publishing. doi:10.1887/0852742622.

Begley, S. (2007). *Change Your Mind, Change Your Brain: How a New Science Reveals Our Extraordinary Potential to Transform Ourselves.* New York, NY: Random House.

Bregman, R. (2020). *Humankind: A hopeful history*. New York, USA: Little, Brown and Company.

Boaler, J. (2019). *Limitless mind: Learn, lead, and live without barriers*. New York, USA: HarperOne Publishers.

Bohm, D. (1980). Wholeness and the Implicate Order. London, UK: Routledge.

Bohm, D., & Peat, F. D. (2010). Science, Order, and Creativity. London, UK: Routledge.

Bourgeault, C. (2020). *Eye of the Heart: A Spiritual Journey into the Imaginal Realm*. Colorado, USA: Shambhala.

Brach, T. (2020). Radical Compassion: Learning to Love Yourself and Your World with the Practice of RAIN. London, UK: RIDER.

Brach, T. (2021). Trusting the Gold: Uncovering Your Natural Goodness. Colorado, USA: Sounds True.

Brackett, M. (2019). Permission to Feel: Unlock the Power of Emotions to Help Yourself and Your Children Thrive. London, UK: Quercus.

Brooks, J. G., and M. G. Brooks. (1999). *In Search of Understanding: The Case for Constructivist Classrooms* (2nd ed.). Alexandria, VA: Association for Supervision and Curriculum Development.

Buckingham, M., & Goodall, A. (2019). *Nine lies about work: A freethinking leader's guide to the real world*. Massachusetts, USA: Harvard Business Review Press.

Burnison, G. (2020). *Leadership U: Accelerating Through the Crisis Curve*. New Jersey, USA: Wiley.

Cain, S. (2013). *Quiet: The Power of Introverts in a World That Can't Stop Talking*. New York, NY: Broadway Books.

Cain, S. (2022). *Bittersweet: How Sorrow and Longing Make Us Whole*. New York, USA: Crown.

Cain, S. (2024). *A Quiet Life in 7 Steps*. New Jersey, USA: Audible Originals.

Catherine, S. (2024). *The jhanas: A practical guide to deep meditative states*. Massachusetts, USA: Wisdom Publications.

Chödrön, P. (2023). How We Live Is How We Die. Colorado, USA: Shambhala.

Chopra, D. (2023). *Quantum Body: The New Science of Living a Longer, Healthier, More Vital Life*. London, UK: Rider.

Church, D. (2020). *Bliss Brain: The Neuroscience of Remodeling Your Brain for Resilience, Creativity, and Joy*. California, USA: Hay House.

Clark, L. (2016). *Beautiful failures*. New South Wales, Australia: Embury

Collins, M. (2022). *The Restorative Spirit: Illuminating the Soul in a Time of Global Awakening*. UK: Transformocene.

Craft, A., Gardner, H., and G. Claxton (Eds.). (2008). *Creativity, Wisdom and Trusteeship: Exploring the*

Role of Education. Thousand Oaks, CA: Corwin Press.

Csikszentmihalyi, M. (2008). *Flow: The Psychology of Optimal Experience* New York: Harper Perennial.

Currivan, J. (2023). *The Story of Gaia: The Big Breath and the Evolutionary Journey of Our Conscious Planet.* Vermont, USA: Inner Traditions.

Dabrowski, K. (with A. Kawczak and M. M. Piechowski). (1970). *Mental Growth through Positive Disintegration.* London: Gryf Publications.

Dabrowski, K. (1972). *Psychoneuroses Is Not an Illness.* London: Gryf Publications.

Dabrowski, K. (1977). *Theory of Levels of Emotional Development (vol. 1)—Multilevelness and Positive Disintegration.* New York: Dabor Science Publications.

Damasio, A. (2005). *Descartes Error: Emotion, Reason, and the Human Brain.* London: Penguin Books.

David, S. (2016). Emotional Agility: Get Unstuck, Embrace Change, and Thrive in Work and Life. New York, USA: Avery.

Davidson, R., & Begley, S. (2012). *The emotional life of your brain: How its unique patterns affect the way you think, feel, and live—and how you can change them.* New York, USA: Hudson Street Press.

Dewey, J. (1963). *Experience and Education.* New York: Collier Books.

Dewey, J. (1997). *Democracy and education: An introduction to the philosophy of education.* New York, USA: Free Press.

Dweck, C. S. (2007). *Mindset: The new psychology of success.* New York, NY: Random House.

Edelman, G. M., and G. Tononi. (2001). *A Universe of Consciousness: How Matter Becomes Imagination.* New York: Basic Books Inc.

Edelman, S. (2013). *Chang Your Thinking,* (3rd ed.). Australia: ABC Books.

Eisenstein, C. (2013). The More Beautiful World Our Hearts Know Is Possible. California, USA: North Atlantic Books.

Epstein, D. (2019). *Range: Why generalists triumph in a specialised world.* New York, USA: Riverhead Books.

Farrell, S. (2023). *A New Universal Dream: My Journey from Silicon Valley to a Life in Service to Humanity.* Light on Light Press.

Feinstein, D., & Eden, D. (2024). *Tapping: Self-healing with the transformative power of energy psychology.* Colorado, USA: Sounds True.

Fischer, N., & Moon, S. (2016). *What is Zen?: Plain talk for a beginner's mind.* Colorado, USA: Shambhala

Frankl, V. E. (2006). *Man's search for meaning: The classic tribute to hope from the Holocaust.* London, UK: Rider.

Fredrickson, B. (2009). *Positivity: Ground-breaking Research Reveals How to Embrace the Hidden Strength of Positive Emotions, Overcome Negativity, and Thrive*. New York, NY: Crown.

Gardner, H. (2006). *Multiple Intelligences: New Horizons*. New York: Basic Books.

Garfinkel, P. (2024). *Becoming Gandhi: My Experiment Living the Mahatma's 6 Moral Truths in Immoral Times*. Colorado, USA: Sounds True.

Gates, N. (2016). *A Brain for Life: How to Optimise Your Brain's Health by Making Simple Lifestyle Changes Now*. Sydney, Australia: HarperCollins Publishers.

Goldberg, E. (2001). *The Executive Brain: Frontal Lobes and the Civilised Mind* (Vol. XIX). New York: Oxford University Press.

Goldstein, J. (2013). Insight meditation: The practice of freedom. Colorado, USA: Shambhala.

Goldstein, J., & Kornfield, J. (2001). *Seeking the Heart of Wisdom: The Path of Insight Meditation*. Colorado, USA: Shambhala Publications.

Goleman, D. (2005). *Emotional Intelligence*. New York: Bantam Books.

Goleman, D. (2013). *Focus: The Hidden Driver of Excellence*. New York, NY: HarperCollins.

Goleman, D. (2006). *Social intelligence: The revolutionary new science of human relationships*. New York: Bantam.

Goleman, D. & Davidson, R. (2017). *Altered Traits: Science Reveals How Meditation Changes Your Mind, Brain, and Body*. New York: Avery.

Goleman, D., and P. Senge. (2014). *The Triple Focus*. Northampton, MA: More Than Sound.

Grant, A. (2021). Think Again: The Power of Knowing What You Don't Know. London, UK: WH ALLEN.

Gregersen, H. (2018). *Questions Are the Answer: A Breakthrough Approach to Your Most Vexing Problems at Work and in Life*. New York, NY: Harper Business.

Grof, S. (1988). *The Adventure of Self-Discovery: Dimensions of Consciousness and New Perspectives in Psychotherapy and Inner Exploration*. New York, USA: SUNY Press.

Gunaratana, H. (2011). *Mindfulness in Plain English*. Massachusetts, USA: Wisdom Publications.

Gunaratana, H., & Ziegler, V. (2024). *Dependent origination in plain English.* Massachusetts, USA: Wisdom Publications.

Halifax, J. (2019). Standing at the Edge: Finding Freedom Where Fear and Courage Meet. New York, USA: Flatiron Books.

Halifax, J. (2029). *Being with Dying: Cultivating Compassion and Fearlessness in the Presence of Death*. Colorado, USA: Shambhala.

Hanh, T. N. (2011). True love: A practice for awakening the heart. Colorado, USA: SHAMBHALA.

Hanh, T. N. (2017). The Art of Living. London, UK: RIDER.

Hanson, R. (2013). *Hardwiring happiness: The new brain science of contentment, calm, and confidence.* New York, NY: Harmony.

Hanson, R. (2018). *Resilient: How to Grow an Unshakable Core of Calm, Strength, and Happiness.* **New York, USA: Harmony.**

Hanson, R. (2020). Neurodharma: New science, ancient wisdom, and seven practices of the highest happiness. New York, USA: Crown.

Hanson, R. and R. Mendius. (2009). *Buddha's brain: The practical neuroscience of happiness, love & wisdom.* Oakland, CA: New harbinger Publications.

Harari, Y. N. (2018). 21 Lessons for the 21st Century. New York, USA: Spiegel & Grau.

Hayashi, A. (2020). *Social presencing theater: The art of making a true move.* Massachusetts, USA: PI Press.

Hayes, S. C. (2019). A Liberated Mind: How to Pivot Toward What Matters. New York, USA: Avery.

Hofmann, S. G., Hayes, S. C., & Lorscheid, D. N. (2021). Learning Process-Based Therapy: A Skills Training Manual for Targeting the Core Processes of Psychological Change in Clinical Practice. California, USA: New Harbinger Publications.

Hübl, T. (2024). Attuned: Practicing Interdependence to Heal Our Trauma—and Our World. Colorado, USA: Sounds True.

Huffington, A. (2016). *The sleep revolution: Transforming your life, one night at a time.* New York, USA: Harmony Books.

Jain, S. (2022). Healing ourselves: Biofield science and the future of health. Colorado, USA: Sounds True.

Jinpa, T. (2005). *Mind training: The great collection.* Massachusetts, USA: Wisdom Publications.

Jung, C. G. (2023). *The Theory of Psychoanalysis.* Illinois, USA: Lushena Books.

Jung, C. G. (Author), & Shamdasani, S. (Editor). (2013). *The Red Book: A reader's edition.* New York: USA Norton agency titles.

Doty, J. R. (2016). Into the Magic Shop: A Neurosurgeon's Quest to Discover the Mysteries of the Brain and the Secrets of the Heart. New York, USA: Avery.

Kabat-Zinn, J. (2009). *Full catastrophe living, revised edition: How to cope with stress, pain and illness using mindfulness meditation.* New York, NY: Bantam Books.

Kabat-Zinn, J. (2005). *Wherever You Go, There You Are: Mindfulness Meditation in Everyday Life*, New York: Hachette Books.

Kahn, M. (2019). *Whatever Arises, Love That: A Love Revolution That Begins with You.* Colorado, USA: Sounds True.

Kahneman, D. (2011). *Thinking, fast and slow*. New York, USA: Farrar, Straus and Giroux.

Kaufman, S. B. (2020). Transcend: The new science of self-actualisation. New York, USA :TarcherPerigee.

Kaufman, S. B. & C. Gregoire. (2016). *Wired to Create - Unravelling the Mysteries of the Creative Mind*. USA: Tarcherperigee.

Kaur, V. (2022). *See no stranger: A memoir and manifesto of revolutionary love*. USA: Aster.

Kaza, S. (Ed.). (2020). *A wild love for the world: Joanna Macy and the work of our time*. Colorado, USA: Shambhala.

Kegan, R. (1982). *The evolving self: Problem and process in human development*. Cambridge, MA: Harvard University Press.

Kelly, L. (2019). *The way of effortless mindfulness: A revolutionary guide for living an awakened life*. Colorado, USA: Sounds True.

Keltner, D. (2017). *Awe: The Transformative Power of Everyday Wonder*. New York, USA: Penguin Press.

Klemp, N. (2024). *Open: Living with an Expansive Mind in a Distracted World*. Colorado, USA: Sounds True.

Kofman, F. (2018). *The meaning revolution: The power of transcendent leadership*. New York, USA: Currency.

Kohn, A. (2005). *Unconditional Parenting: Moving from Rewards and Punishments to Love and Reason*. New York, NY: Atria Books.

Kolb, D. (1983). *Experiential Learning: Experience as the Source of Learning and Development.* Upper Saddle River, NJ: Prentice Hall.

Kuntzelman, E., & Robinson, J. (Eds.). (2023). *The Holomovement: Embracing Our Collective Purpose to Unite Humanity.* Light on Light Press.

Langer, E. J. (2015). *Mindfulness*: 25th anniversary edition. Massachusetts, USA: Da Capo Lifelong Books.

Langer, E. J. (2016). *The Power of Mindful Learning.* Massachusetts, USA: Da Capo Lifelong Books.

Langer, E. (2023). *The Mindful Body: Thinking Our Way to Lasting Health.* London, UK: Robinson.

Levitin, D. J. (2007). *This is your brain on music: Understanding a human obsession.* London, UK: Atlantic.

Levitin, D. J. (2014). *The organised mind: Thinking straight in the age of information overload.* New York, USA: Dutton.

Lin, J., Culham, T. E., & Edwards, S. (Eds.). (2019). Contemplative Pedagogies for Transformative Teaching, Learning, and Being. North Carolina, USA: Information Age Publishing.

Lingo, K. J. (2021). *We Were Made for These Times: Ten Lessons on Moving Through Change, Loss, and Disruption.* California, USA: PARALLAX.

Loizzo, J., Brandon, F., Wolf, E. J., & Neale, M. (Eds.). (2023). *Advances in Contemplative Psychotherapy:*

Accelerating Personal and Social Transformation. Philadelphia, USA: Routledge.

Long, J., & Perry, P. (2011). *Evidence of the Afterlife: The Science of Near-Death Experiences.* New York, USA: HarperCollins.

Ludvik, M. J. B. (Ed.). (2016). The Neuroscience of Learning and Development: Enhancing Creativity, Compassion, Critical Thinking, and Peace in Higher Education. Sterling, Virginia: Stylus Publishing.

Macy, J. (1991). *Mutual causality in Buddhism and general systems theory: The dharma of natural systems.* New York, USA: State University of New York Press.

Macy, J. R., & Johnstone, C. (2012). Active Hope: How to Face the Mess We're in without Going Crazy. California, USA: New World Library.

Manuel, Z. E. (2023). Opening to Darkness: Eight Gateways for Being with the Absence of Light in Unsettling Times. Colorado, USA: Shambhala.

Maslow, A. (1968). *Toward a Psychology of Being.* New York: Van Nostrand Reinhold.

Maslow, A. (1993). *Farther Reaches of Human Nature.* New York: Arkana.

Maté, G. (2024). *The Myth of Normal: Trauma, Illness & Healing in a Toxic Culture.* London, UK: VERMILION.

Maull, F. (2019). *Radical Responsibility: How to Move Beyond Blame, Fearlessly Live Your Highest*

Purpose, and Become an Unstoppable Force for Good. Colorado, USA: Sounds True.

McGarey, G. (2023). The Well-Lived Life: A 102-Year-Old Doctor's Six Secrets to Health and Happiness at Every Age. London, UK: Michael Joseph.

Miller, L. (2022). *The Awakened Brain: The Psychology of Spirituality and Our Search for Meaning.* New York, USA: Penguin Press.

Naser, S. (2011). A Beautiful Mind. New York, USA: Simon & Schuster.

Neal, J. (2023). *Inspiring Workplace Spirituality*. Leeds, England: Emerald Publishing.

Neff, K., (2011). *Self-compassion: The proven power of being kind to yourself.* New York, NY: HarperCollins.

Nissanka, H. S. S. (1994). Buddhist psychotherapy: An Eastern therapeutical approach to mental problems. Madurai, India: Sangam Books.

Nunez, P. L. (2016). *The new science of consciousness: Exploring the complexity of brain, mind, and self.* New York, USA: Prometheus Books.

Orloff, J. (2019). *Thriving as an empath: 365 days of self-care for sensitive people.* Colorado, USA: Sounds True.

Orloff, J. (2024). *The Genius of Empathy: Practical Skills to Heal Your Sensitive Self, Your Relationships, and the World.* Colorado, USA: Sounds True.

Owen-Smith, P. (2017). *Contemplative Mind in the Scholarship of Teaching and Learning*. Indiana, USA: Indiana University Press.

Palmer, K., & Blake, D. (2018). *The expertise economy: How the smartest companies use learning to engage, compete, and succeed*. London, England; Massachusetts, USA: Nicholas Brealey Publishing.

Palmer, P. J., and A. Zajonc (2010). *The Heart of Higher Education: A Call to Renewal*. San Francisco, CA: Jossey-Bass.

Papadopoulos, R. K. (Ed.). (2006). The Handbook of Jungian Psychology—Theory, Practice and Applications. Sussex, UK: Routledge.

Patten, T. (2018). A New Republic of the Heart: An Ethos for Revolutionaries--A Guide to Inner Work for Holistic Change. California, USA: North Atlantic Books.

Paul, R., and L. Elder, L. (2000). *Critical Thinking: Tools for Taking Charge of Your Learning and Your Life*. Upper Saddle River, NJ: Pearson Education.

Piechowski, M. M. (2006). *Mellow Out, They Say. If I Only Could: Intensities and Sensitivities of the Young and Bright*. Madison, WI: Yunasa Books.

Pink, D. (2009). *Drive: The Surprising Truth About What Motivates Us*. New York: Riverhead.

Piirto, J. (2004) *Understanding Creativity*. Scottsdale: Great Potential.

Porges, S. W., & Porges, S. (2023). *Our Polyvagal World: How Safety and Trauma Change Us*. New York, USA: Norton agency titles.

Prendergast, J. J. (2019). *The Deep Heart: Our Portal to Presence*. Colorado, USA: Sounds True.

Rankin, L. (2022). *Sacred Medicine: A Doctor's Quest to Unravel the Mysteries of Healing*. Colorado, USA: Sounds True.

Rock, D. (2009). *Your Brain at Work: Strategies for Overcoming Distraction, Regaining Focus, and Working Smarter All Day Long*, Harper Business, New York.

Rudd, R. (2022). *The art of contemplation: A gentle path to wholeness and prosperity*. Devon, UK: Gene Keys Publishing.

Salzberg, S. (1995). *Loving kindness: The revolutionary art of happiness*. Boston, MA: Shambhala.

Salzberg, S. (2023). Real Life: The Journey from Isolation to Openness and Freedom. New York, USA: Flatiron Books.

Sapolsky, R. M. (2017). *Behave: The biology of humans at our best and worst*. New York, USA: Penguin Press.

Schairer, S. J. (2023). *A case for compassion: What happens when we prioritize people and the planet.* Washington, D.C., USA: New Degree Press.

Scharmer, C. O. (2018). *Theory U: Leading from the Future as It Emerges*. California, USA: Berrett-Koehler Publishers.

Schmidt, A. (2005). *Dipa Ma: The life and legacy of a Buddhist master*. New York, USA: BlueBridge.

Senge, P. (2006). *The Fifth Discipline: The Art & Practice of the Learning Organization*. New York, USA: Doubleday.

Shigeoka, S. (2024). *Seek: How Curiosity Can Transform Your Life and Change the World*. London, UK: Bluebird.

Siegal, D. (2011). *Mindsight: Transform Your Brain with the New Science of Kindness*. UK: Oneworld Publications.

Siegel D. J. (2014). *Brainstorm: The Power and Purpose of the Teenage Brain*. New York, NY: Tarcher Perigee.

Siegel, D. (2020). *Aware: The Science and Practice of Presence--The Groundbreaking Meditation Practice*. New York, NY: TarcherPerigee.

Siegel, D. J. (2020). *The Developing Mind: How Relationships and the Brain Interact to Shape Who We Are*. New York, USA: Guilford Press.

Siegel, D. J. (2022*). IntraConnected: MWe (Me + We) as the Integration of Self, Identity, and Belonging*. New York, USA: Norton.

Siegel, D. J., & Bryson, T. P. (2011). The Whole-Brain Child: Revolutionary Strategies to Nurture Your Child's Developing Mind. New York, USA: Delacorte Press.

Siegel, D. J., & Bryson, T. P. (2018). *The yes brain: How to cultivate courage, curiosity, and resilience in your child*. New York, USA: Bantam Books.

Silverman, L. K. (2002). *Upside-Down Brilliance: The Visual-Spatial Learner.* Denver, CO: DeLeon Publishing.

Simons, N. (2022). *Nature, culture and the sacred: A woman listens for leadership.* Massachusetts, USA: Green Fire Press.

Singer, M. A. (2022). *Living Untethered: Beyond the Human Predicament.* California, USA: New Harbinger.

Smith, E. E. (2017). *The power of meaning: Crafting a life that matters.* New York, USA: Crown Publishing Group.

Sofer, O. J. (2018). *Say what you mean: A mindful approach to nonviolent communication.* Colorado, USA: Shambhala.

Sofer, O. J. (2023). *Your Heart Was Made for This: Contemplative Practices for Meeting a World in Crisis with Courage, Integrity, and Love.* Colorado, USA: Shambhala Publications.

Sousa, D. A. (2011). *How the Brain Learns* (4th ed.), Thousand Oaks, CA: Corwin.

Suzuki, S. (2020). *Zen Mind, Beginner's Mind: 50th Anniversary Edition.* Colorado, USA: Shambhala.

Tan, C. (2014). Search Inside Yourself: The Unexpected Path to Achieving Success, Happiness (and World Peace). San Francisco: CA, USA: Harper One.

Taylor, A. (2024). *Higher Ground: How Business Can Do the Right Thing in a Turbulent World.* Massachusetts, USA: Harvard Business Review Press.

Teasdale, W. (2001). *The Mystic Heart: Discovering a Universal Spirituality in the World's Religions.* California, USA: New World Library.

Tift, B. (2019). *Already free: Buddhism meets psychotherapy on the path of liberation.* Colorado, USA: Sounds True.

Tolle, E. (2018). *The Power of Now: A Guide to Spiritual Enlightenment.* New South Wales, Australia: Hachette Australia.

Tulving, E. (1972). Episodic and semantic memory. In E. Tulving, W. Donaldson & G. H. Bower (Eds.). *Organisation of memory* (pp. 381-403). New York: Academic Press.

van der Kolk, B. (2015). *The Body Keeps the Score: Mind, Brain and Body in the Transformation of Trauma.* New York, USA: Penguin Press.

Volf, M., Croasmun, M., & McAnnally-Linz, R. (2023). *A Life Worth Living: A Guide to What Matters Most.* London, UK: Rider.

Walker, M. (2018). *Why We Sleep: The New Science of Sleep and Dreams,* USA: Penguin Books.

Wekelo, K. A. (2021). *Culture infusion: 9 principles for creating and maintaining a thriving organisational culture.* Georgia, USA: Stress-Free Kids.

Weston, J. (2023). *Fierce Civility: Transforming Our Global Culture from Polarization to Lasting Peace.* Independently Published.

White, R. C. (2009). *A. Lincoln: A biography*. New York, NY: Random House.

Wilber, K. (2001). A Theory of Everything: An Integral Vision for Business, Politics, Science & Spirituality. Colorado, USA: Shambhala

Williams, M., & Penman, D. (2011). *Mindfulness: A practical guide to finding peace in a frantic world*. London, England: Piatkus.

Williamson, M. (2023.). *The mystic Jesus: The mind of love*. USA: HarperCollins.

Yetunde, P. A. (2023). Casting Indra's Net: Fostering Spiritual Kinship and Community. Colorado, USA: Shambhala.

Zull, J. E. (2002). *The Art of Changing the Brain: Enriching the Practice of Teaching by Exploring the Biology of Learning*. Sterling, Virginia, USA: Stylus Publishing.

Zull, J. E. (2011). *From Brain to Mind: Using Neuroscience to Guide Change in Education*. Sterling, Virginia, USA: Stylus Publishing.

Websites and organisations that influenced me (the author)

https://banyantogether.com/

https://bethosmer.com/

https://casel.org/

https://ccare.stanford.edu/ (The Centre for Compassion and Altruism Research and Education)

https://centerforhumanpotential.com/

https://centerhealthyminds.org/

https://charterforcompassion.org/

https://chicenter.com/

https://choprafoundation.org/

https://conorneill.com/

https://craighamiltonglobal.com/

https://dianepooleheller.com/

https://drdansiegel.com/

https://drgabormate.com/

https://drhyman.com/

https://drjudithorloff.com/

https://drsuemorter.com/

https://eckharttolle.com/

https://edgewalkers.org/

https://eftuniverse.com/

https://evolutionarycollective.com/

https://fetzer.org/

https://foodrevolution.org/

https://genekeys.com/

https://ggsc.berkeley.edu/   (Greater Good Science Centre)

https://greggbraden.com/

https://hbr.org/ (Harvard Business Review)

https://jackkornfield.com/

https://jungplatform.com/

https://kellyblaser.com/

https://lynnemctaggart.com/

https://marclesser.net/

https://marianne.com/

https://mariashriver.com

https://mattkahn.org/

https://meditativestory.com/

https://mindandlife-europe.org/

https://mindfulness.com/

https://mindsightinstitute.com/

https://missionjoy.org/

https://nalandainstitute.org/

https://noetic.org/ (Institute of Noetic Sciences)

https://pocketproject.org/

https://positivepsychology.com/

https://rickhanson.com/

https://sangha.live/

https://scottbarrykaufman.com/

https://strozziinstitute.org/

https://susancain.net/

https://tergar.org/

https://terryreal.com/

https://thefourwinds.com/

https://thenaturallaw.com/

https://theshiftnetwork.com/

https://thomashuebl.com/

https://thus.org/ (Tibet House US)

https://tricycle.org/

https://valariekaur.com/

https://wisdomexperience.org/

https://womancenteredcoaching.com/

https://yestosuccess.com/

https://youryearofmiracles.com/

https://zivameditation.com/

https://www.alexiscohen.org/

https://www.andrewharvey.net/

https://www.awakenedself.com/

https://www.bcorporation.net/en-us/

https://www.brucelipton.com/

https://www.centerforcompassionateleadership.org/

https://www.chi.is/ (The Consciousness and Healing Initiative)

https://www.compassionateleaderscircle.com/

https://www.consciouscapitalism.org/

https://www.consciousmarketer.com/

https://www.dharma.org/ (Insight Meditation Society)

https://www.dharmamoon.com/

https://www.drchristopherwillard.com/

https://www.energypsych.org/

https://www.gaia.com/

https://www.garrisoninstitute.org/

https://www.globalcompassioncoalition.org/

https://www.happinesssangha.com/

https://www.health.harvard.edu/

https://www.heartmath.org/

https://www.heartmind.co/

https://www.holstee.com/

https://www.humanitysteam.org/

https://www.lionsroar.com/

https://www.lovewhatmatters.com/

https://www.marymorrissey.com/

https://www.meawisdom.com/

https://www.mindandlife.org/

https://www.mindful.org/

https://www.nicabm.com/ (National Institute for Clinical and Behavioural Medicine)

https://www.orenjaysofer.com/

https://www.pamelaayoyetunde.com/

https://www.rachaelomeara.com/

https://www.relationallifefoundation.org

https://www.shamashalidina.com/

https://www.sharonsalzberg.com/

https://www.soundstrue.com/

https://www.spiritualityandpractice.com/

https://www.tarabrach.com/

https://www.tenpercent.com/

https://www.thetappingsolution.com/

https://www.timeofthesixthsun.com/

https://www.upaya.org/

https://www.wisdomforlife.life/

https://www.wisdom2summit.com/

https://www.wisebrain.org/ (The Wellspring Institute for Neuroscience and Contemplative Wisdom)

https://www.worldhappiness.academy/

https://www.younity.one/

Author Bio

Dr Chandana Watagodakumbura has been in academia for over twenty-five years, teaching in ICT, IS, computer science, engineering, management, and education. He contributed to some development and conducting of over 70 courses in higher education. He has PhD, Master's, and BSc degrees in engineering and a Graduate Certificate (Higher Education) from RMIT University, the University of Peradeniya, and Monash University.

More recently, he has undergone training and education on Emotional Intelligence (Goleman EI), Compassionate Integrity (Life University), Inner MBA (Sounds True/LinkedIn/Wisdom 2.0/NYU), iCHANGE: Introduction to Social Innovation (Education Queensland/CQUniversity), u.lab: Leading from the Emerging Future – U Theory (edX), Interpersonal Neurobiology (Mindsight Institute), Living Beautifully: Transformative Science and Mindfulness Practices to Cultivate a Wise Heart (Mindsight Institute),

Self-Actualisation Coaching (Centre for Human Potential) and Transformational Experience Design (Sutra).

Chandan's longstanding broad interest in education and human development led him to inquire, explore and self-publish two books titled "Education from a Deeper and Multidisciplinary Perspective: For a Sustainable Development of the Neurodiverse Society" and "Programming the Brain: Educational Neuroscience Perspective: Pedagogical Practices and Study Skills for Enhanced Learning and Metacognition" previously.

Chandana is currently a visiting academic at CQUniversity. He has also worked at RMIT and Monash Universities, the University of Peradeniya, and the University of Northern Virginia (Cyprus campus). Since September 2020, Chandana has been serving as a member of the Harvard Business Review (HBR) Advisory Council.

About the book

"Broadening Our Focus for Healing and Growth: by Enhancing Consciousness and Spaciousness" attempts to highlight the additional dimension of broadening or opening our senses available for us for our healing and growth. The journeys of healing and growth are not separate; they are interwoven, and one feeds to the other. We can broaden our focus, starting from ourselves and extending to immediate and broader communities and even to planetary and cosmic levels. The broader the focus, the better outcomes on individual and collective well-being. With the appreciation of such vast interconnectedness and holomovement, we inherently become loving and compassionate beings contributing positively to evolving consciousness. With an extensive bibliography and links to other resources, this short read brings forth the author's subjective, direct experiences, intuitive knowledge, and supporting conciliant evidence from science and various other sources. It discusses six emergent areas of the topic: relationships, inquiry into consciousness, whole-person development, contemplative practices and pedagogies, learning informally and experientially and some neural basis of learning, healing and expanding consciousness and spaciousness.